554

ROGERS HALL
LOWELL, MASS.

BY EDWARD WEEKS

THIS TRADE OF WRITING

THE OPEN HEART

Edited by Edward Weeks

GREAT SHORT NOVELS

THE POCKET ATLANTIC

The Open Heart

The Open Heart

by

EDWARD WEEKS

An Atlantic Monthly Press Book
BOSTON · Little, Brown and Company · TORONTO

LIBRARY OF CONGRESS CATALOG CARD NO. 55–10760

Seventh Printing

The author wishes to thank the following for permission to reprint selections which appear in this volume: Sir Osbert Sitwell — for permission to reprint from a letter to Edward Weeks. H. M. Tomlinson — for permission to reprint from a letter to Edward Weeks. E. B. White — for permission to reprint selections from ONE MAN'S MEAT and THE SECOND TREE FROM THE CORNER.
Also: The *Atlantic Monthly.* The *Boston Herald.* The *Ford Times.* Harcourt, Brace and Company, Inc. — for permission to reprint from THE SECOND COMMON READER by Virginia Woolf. Harper & Brothers — for permission to reprint selections from INNOCENTS ABROAD by Mark Twain; from THE LOVE LETTERS OF MARK TWAIN, edited by Dixon Wecter; and from ONE MAN'S MEAT and THE SECOND TREE FROM THE CORNER by E. B. White. Harvard University Press — for permission to reprint selections from THE LETTERS AND PRIVATE PAPERS OF WILLIAM MAKEPEACE THACKERAY, collected and edited by Gordon N. Ray. Houghton Mifflin Company — for permission to reprint selections from THE EDUCATION OF HENRY ADAMS by Henry Adams. The Macmillan Company — for permission to reprint selections from THE NAME AND NATURE OF POETRY by A. E. Housman. The *New Yorker* — for permission to reprint selections from THE SECOND TREE FROM THE CORNER. The *Saturday Review.* Charles Scribner's Sons — for permission to reprint selections from EDITOR TO AUTHOR by Maxwell E. Perkins.

ATLANTIC–LITTLE, BROWN BOOKS
ARE PUBLISHED BY
LITTLE, BROWN AND COMPANY
IN ASSOCIATION WITH
THE ATLANTIC MONTHLY PRESS

Published simultaneously in Canada
by Little, Brown & Company (Canada) Limited

PRINTED IN THE UNITED STATES OF AMERICA

For My Mother
Frederika Suydam Weeks
for her zest and faith

Acknowledgments

There are times when an editor needs encouragement quite as much as a writer, and my encouragement, for which I am truly grateful, came from Miss Virginia Albee, Miss Louise Desaulniers, Mrs. Emily P. Flint, Miss Penelope Greenough, Miss Margaret Mutch and Miss Nancy E. Reynolds, and from Donald B. Snyder, Charles W. Morton and Walter Lippmann.

Contents

[xi   ]

Contents

[xii]

I
New Jersey Boyhood

I

The City

To a boy growing up in the suburbs of New York in the early 1900's the city had the drawing power of a gigantic magnet. Every visit was to see something special, and afterwards the event lived on in your mind. Even the approach was exciting: the train deposited you in the great, lofty, smoke-filled train shed of the Pennsy, and then with your parents you hurried, you ran, down the platform and into the timbered ferryhouse (this was before Mr. McAdoo had finished the Tunnel), watching out for the horse-drawn drays which were being driven onto the lower deck. A boy's place was forward on the top deck, pressed against the rail, where you could see everything in the harbor and, looking up, the pilot in his little house. The wind was sharp, the skyscrapers gleamed in the winter sunlight, and as you crossed the water the ferry would hoot at a passing tug and the tug hooted back; then you came wedging into the slip, with the timbers groaning and the cable wheels clanking melodiously as the ferry made fast.

You might be bound for the Museum of Natural History with its glass cabinets of animals and tiny ancient people. Or for the Hudson Fulton Celebration, that swarming river parade which I watched from the deck of the U.S.S. *New York.* (My Uncle Ray was one of her officers.) As the excursion boats filed by, the White Fleet fired off blank charges, and I remember a wad from one of our guns arching over the brief interval of water into the lap of an excursionist, a fat woman in a basket hat, who became so agitated that she and her campstool collapsed. Or you might be going to the Hippodrome to see *The Fall of Port Arthur,* with wounded men toppling into the water and never coming up. Later the chorus girls in spangles walked right down the stairs into that tank, and they didn't come up either. Every chandelier of the Hippodrome held more electric bulbs than we had in our entire house, as I announced to Mother in a voice that carried. On the back of each seat was a metal slot machine which released a box of chocolates when a coin was inserted. We needed these for my cousin, Alan Church, who let out a wail when the Gatling guns went off at Port Arthur and thereafter was voiceless only when he had a candy in his mouth.

The great trip with Dad was in September to see the Giants play the Athletics in the World Series. Lunch first at the Merchants' Club, with Meringue Chantilly for dessert; then the jammed, feverish ride on the Elevated to the Polo Grounds. You found your seats in the good-natured tumult; you noticed the bunting and flags, Muggsy McGraw going down to coach at third, Christy Mathewson warming up in the box, and "Chief" Meyers behind the plate. It turned cold when the sun went down, and Dad showed Rufus and me how to fold newspapers inside our coats to keep warm.

[4]

The City

Came the year when you went in on your own. Now you were buying your own clothes on an allowance of twenty dollars a month, and I can remember as if it were yesterday the pearl-gray double-breasted, the lavender socks, and the razor-tipped cordovan low shoes which were my first investment. I went to see Hobey Baker play against Harvard in the old St. Nicholas rink, and stood up on my hockey skates all through the last period so that I could be one of the first on the hallowed ice when the game was over. I saw Montgomery and Stone in *Chin Chin* ("Good-by, Girls, I'm Through"); I saw the Vernon Castles do the Castle Walk, and heard Joseph Cawthorne and Julia Sanderson in *The Sunshine Girl* ("You Can't Play Every Instrument in the Band"); I dropped in with apparent casualness for a chop at Keen's Chop House, and the smell of beer was so saturating that I hoped the family would notice it when I got home. By such milestones do we grow up.

2

The Little Gentlemen

MARCH was the fag end and there was nothing much you could do about it; this was the glum month in which we and our teacher began our weary toil through *Ivanhoe*. March was the month for dentistry, an ordeal in which the only kind words were "Now rinse, please"; it was a month in which, if you were a good Episcopalian, you gave up candy for Lent; it was a time when in my part of New Jersey the rain and the mud made indoor sport a boy's only hope.

School with its homework kept us in drudgery for the first five days of the week, but on Friday the servitude began to let up. On Friday afternoon came dancing school. You couldn't exactly call this sport, but it was different from what we had been doing and to that extent better. We met in Arcanum Hall, a vast shiny lodge room with a number of big plush chairs on the dais where the mothers of the girls sat — the mothers of the boys, having less at stake, were infrequent.

We — the Little Gentlemen, as we were called — entered in our twinkling pumps from our separate dressing room; one by one we bowed to Miss Emma Florence, who stood graciously in the center of that vast slippery floor, and then took our seats side by side in the stag row. The young ladies made their entrance, each dropping a curtsy, while we looked on with what might be described as mild interest.

There were no crushes in this business. But once you got going it wasn't too bad. The two Miss Florences in their mauve sateens had a party air and perfume about them; and what is more, they knew how to teach. Boys on one side, girls on the other, we went through the simple exercises, warming up as we got into "Heel-toe-and-a-one-two-three"; and then, when Miss Emma said, "The Young Gentlemen will please take partners for the schottische," there was a scramble for the girls' camp. No love whatever was involved: we chose our partners for their speed, and Marjorie, who was just as skinny as I, I could trust to hold me up as we took the corners.

The waltz and the polka were the best because they worked up so easily into a race. The piano tinkled and round we twirled faster and faster, tongues out, curls flying, elbows all set, impervious to dizziness and the freshly waxed floor, past Bud, past Hump, faster and faster until with a click of the castanets Miss Florence silenced the piano and we all lurched to a stop with a look of elation as we heard her say, "The Young Gentlemen are going too fast."

For Saturday afternoons Keith's Vaudeville was one of those objectives which we didn't discuss at home. Just said we were going out. The trouble with our particular Keith's was that it had such a strong smell of disinfectants. I would overlook this between visits, but I couldn't overlook it when I was in my seat. Because of the smell and the inevitability of a lemon or two in the acts, we very seldom sat through the entire show twice — besides, we had to save time for a Hot Dusty on the way home. A Hot Dusty, as served at our favorite soda counter, consisted of vanilla ice cream coated with a thick dusting of malted milk; over the pyramid was then poured hot melted fudge in which were walnuts and pecans, with a dab of marshmallow whip on the top — total cost, fifteen cents. It was consumed with slow intensity and a gradual feeling of surfeit. Home cooking after a Hot Dusty was tasteless. And next day there were cankers.

3
Picnic in the Rain

LOOKING back on it, a picnic gone wrong is about the most rueful experience in the so-called world of pleasure. For this, one must blame the caprice of nature but even more that stubborn optimism which settles on those who are determined to picnic. The food can be ordered, guests invited, site chosen, husband placated days in advance, but the one thing you cannot order is the weather. If a northeaster sets in, you call things off; it is the lowering, overcast day that leads you astray.

I have known some mighty fine picnics and more that weren't, but the most humiliating I can remember was an expedition from our suburb in New Jersey to Bronx Park in May, 1910. It was organized by my Aunt Hattie as a birthday party for my cousin Katherine and six of her classmates; the girls were a little older than I — I was twelve — and I knew I had been included because I wouldn't take liberties and might be a help.

We got off to an ominous start. It looked like rain but nothing could daunt Aunt Hattie's optimism, and so the nine of us gathered punctually at the railroad station, where I was put in charge of the wicker lunch basket. I was too inexperienced to realize that you never carry a picnic basket by its handle; and as I followed the girls up into the day coach I tripped on the top step, lurched forward into the car and out into the aisle, and under the seats poured the hard-boiled eggs, the chicken and jam sandwiches, the pickles and cupcakes — some wrapped, some not. I had barely retrieved our cindery repast by the time we reached Newark, and by then it was raining.

Rain streaked the windows all the way into New York and all the long way uptown on the Elevated. "Rain before seven, clear before eleven," said someone cheerily. (But what about after eleven?) When we reached the Bronx Zoo it was still raining hard, which meant that we had to run from cover to cover. I was now carrying the lunch basket in both arms, and my first chance to set it down was in the monkey house. This, of course, was in the days when the intimacy between animal and spectator was more sensitive than Dr. Fairfield Osborn now permits. Rain will do wonders for the *esprit de corps* of a monkey house, and there they were frisking, flea-picking, and fondling in an atmosphere of undiluted monkey.

The rain never let up, so at one o'clock I was sent out to find a cave, some sheltered spot where we could breathe and eat our lunch. Had we thought to ask the Director, he might have provided us with an empty cage, but this idea never occurred. Instead I found a dank opening in the rocks where, if you sat on your raincoat, it wasn't quite as wet as sitting in the open. We ate in silence, punctured by the steady drip.

After lunch — still with that darn wicker basket — we made a dash for the next house, which happened to contain the larger mammals — elephants, hippos, and the rhinoceroses. They, too, it appeared, had eaten, and now they were digesting, copiously. This was a lesson in anatomy not to be missed. "Come, girls," said Aunt Hattie, "let's move on." And we did, out into the wet. We saw the snakes, the birds of Oriental plumage, and the big cats — and at 3:30, thank the Lord, we started for home! It was still raining.

I could speak of other picnics in which the unpredictable occurred: the Oxford picnic on the banks of the Isis where, in the circle of English friends, I had my wind knocked out by a sharp blow to the solar plexus delivered by my intended because I had triflingly removed a cigarette from her lips; the Sedgwick family picnic on Crane's Beach where the men at the four corners of the beach blanket, armed with relays of cigars, were just able to keep the mosquitoes out of the food; and that happy expedition to remote Plum Island where I locked the keys inside the car and spent the rest of the daylight trying to fish them out with a twisted wire coat hanger. You don't have to depend on rain.

4

Hero Worship

PRINCETON is a lovely spot in the spring and to a prep-school boy a place for hero worship. I used to go down religiously on the 9:01 every Saturday after May 1. My mother insisted on my carrying a box lunch. I of course was heartily ashamed of it, hid it under the seat, and left it there as I scuttled off at the Junction. Why worry? One of my heroes would feed me at his club.

Immediately on arrival I would buy a copy of the *Daily Princetonian* and dope out my schedule for the day. Here one Saturday morning I watched an extravagant game of baseball between the Princeton *Tiger* and the Harvard *Lampoon.* There was a keg of beer beside first base and a dipper for anyone who made it safely. The Harvard idiots had brought along a little truck with four rubber-tire wheels, which they strapped on the rear of the base runner. With this contraption the poor fish tried to steal second, and I remember thinking that it must have given him an awful jounce when he hit the ground. The whole thing seemed to me a little disrespectful, so I moved on to the Varsity tennis courts where, squatting on the turf, I watched the singles against Yale.

The baseball game at Commencement was always the

high point. The alumni were back in force, and the class tents brimming with beer and laughter were a wonderful side show for a twelve-year-old who had no business to be there. I had no right there; neither had the beer dogs, those fat, loose-skinned, laughing dogs, part terrier, part anything else, that wandered in from the campus and really lapped up the beer.

After lunch the alumni P-rade lined up and the brass bands began trumpeting the huge serpent into University Field. The very old alumni came in first, then the marshals in their white flannels and blue coats, wearing orange cushions on their heads. The oldest classes had canes and every kind of straw hat, but the younger alumni were in costume — a big brass band, then the class banner, then the pirates and the sheiks and the boys from the Tyrol with outrageous signs that made you giggle. On they came, filling up the bleachers and grandstand. Finally the seniors, a big class, and this was the last you'd see of them.

All the while the Princeton Varsity had been warming up, with the Yale team the first to come to bat, now sitting sardonically in their dugout. The Umps called out the Captains, and you could imagine what they were saying: "If the ball goes into the crowd there, it is a two-base hit, but over the center field fence, that's a homer." And now the Tiger pitcher took the mound and began his warm-up, and you were really trembling. So was the Princeton infield; they always seemed to get the jitters at Commencement. I shall never forget one game in which each of the first five Elis to come to bat, bunted — and four times in succession the infield threw the ball over first's head. It was pathetic. But Princeton got it all back with a homer in the ninth. Game over, you drifted out with the happy crowd and trailed along with the band of Scottish Highlanders until it seemed time to eat.

After supper on Prospect you followed the couples on their way to hear Senior Singing. The seniors sat on their benches in front of Nassau Hall (benches which they would burn the night before graduation); and, though you had often heard the songs they sang, on this particular night, as dark fell and the cigarettes became fireflies and you no longer could pick out the leader or the soloist, the songs seemed to seize you by the throat. They sounded like something deeply felt, those songs — "The Orange and the Black," "Australian Girls," "Going Back to Nassau Hall," "Don't You Hear Dem Bells?", "Safe Now in the Wide, Wide World"; all day long one thing had led to another, but this was something you kept.

So at last it broke up, and you went slowly down through Blair Arch to the tracks. There was always a train and it was always late in starting. And now you had to fight off sleep. You remembered those villainous bunts and the homer, and then as the conductor took your ticket you had the sense to say, "Please be sure to wake me if I fall asleep. I get off at Elizabeth."

5
First Cruise

To a boy bound for the Jersey Coast, summer began with the odor of cinders, sunlight on the red plush seats and the dusty varnish of the P.R.R. daycoach which took you to Point Pleasant. Summer burst into view with your first sight of the ocean seen in the cleft of the dunes, the sunlight sparkling on the water with a million spear-points and the sand so dazzling white. You couldn't face it; you had to squint your eyes at first.

You found the gang at the Yacht Club and in early June the west wind blowing in gusts across the Bay gave you an excuse for wearing your school sweater, inside out of course, with the letter, for modesty's sake, on your back. There were no races yet, for only half the boats were in the water. I remember that afternoon when Beau, Buzz, Mario and I stood in the sand beside Mort Johnson's boatworks regarding the catboat which he had just promised us for a week's cruise. There she sat, on the cradle, out of water, squat and immobile. But once we had put the cabin on and helped with the painting and the paint had dried, she would be ours. For one week. Gosh, you could certainly make Atlantic City in that time. Might even make Cape May.

New Jersey Boyhood

When we had done our work, Mort was as good as his word and better. The *Fat Cat* was ours for a week, and with it a tender. This was to be the first long cruise for any of us, but we laid our plans like old-timers. Mario (he would be seventeen that September) was of course our skipper. Beau, Buzz and I were two years his junior. I can remember the gravity, if not the actual words, with which Mario addressed us.

"Listen, fellers. There's going to be no monkey business about this. I figure it'll take us two days to reach Atlantic City, two days for shore leave, and that gives us a margin even if we have head winds on the way home. We've got to turn the boat back to Mort just as we got her."

From the head of Barnegat Bay it was sixty miles to Atlantic City by the inland waterway, with only two short hauls in the open ocean. Mario had the essential roll of charts; the provisions — canned goods mostly — were stowed in the stern close to the kerosene stove. The blankets and duffel bags were forward, and the ship's purse amounted to $27.80 on Monday morning, the morning of our departure. I forgot to say that the *Fat Cat* measured twenty-two feet at the waterline.

It was a hazy June day when we left with the wind blowing steadily from the north. We ran free, past Mantoloking, past Lavallette; and, hunger smiting us, we put in at Seaside Park for a dollar's worth of the famous Seaside Park buns, thick with brown sugar, currants, pecans, and stickiness. We ate as many as we could, stowed the remainder in the food locker, and headed into unknown waters. Seaside was the furthest we had ever been down the Bay.

We were stripped to the buff, and sunburning as all good mariners should; and I remember that toward the end of the afternoon we made our scrawny appearance in the midst of a fishing fleet which was hauling in weakfish as fast as the hooks could be baited.

"Head her up into the wind," commanded Mario, "and we'll catch some chowder for supper." It wasn't the chowder's fault that supper began for me an uninterrupted week of heartburn; it was the fault of the fried potatoes brown around the edges, cold as flint inside; it was the fault of the stewed tomatoes out of a can and not quite hot; it was the fault of the kerosene stove which I tasted in every bite.

We spent the first night off Beach Haven, which was quite a run; and we drifted to sleep listening to the slap of waves against the hull. At least some did. The cabin was big enough to shelter two sleepers, and the other two slept on the wooden seats in the open cockpit. We drew lots for this, and I lost. Unfortunately I drew that portion of the seat where someone's heel had already broken one of the slats. I remember my hip in the jagged depression, I remember the stars, the damp gathering on my blankets, and my heartburn as regular as a cuckoo clock.

It seemed almost no time at all before Mario ordered us overboard for a dip before breakfast — fried eggs and bacon, weak coffee with lots of condensed milk. And again we were on our way. The wind had shifted to the

[17   ]

northeast, and we still ran free, now across the great expanse of Little Egg Harbor, now through the narrow connecting waterways. We sighted Atlantic City that afternoon, and after a long struggle against the outgoing tide, made the inlet and drew abreast of the Yacht Club. It was getting on toward sundown. We had been tacking against the tide for three hours, and the bright lights overcame caution. Old-timers had told us to keep away from the Yacht Club. It was a dangerous place to be caught in a nor'easter. Much better to go around the point and anchor inside. But we were tired, heartily tired of our own cooking, and eager for the new world to conquer.

"All right, if we tie up here for the night?" asked Mario as he made a perfect landing at the Yacht Club dock. The dock hand looked laconically at our club pennant, and thought it might be. "We'll sleep aboard," we said professionally, put on clean shirts, slicked down the cowlicks, and went ashore. Mario allowed us each two dollars. You could get a steak dinner for a dollar in those days, and for me with my cuckoo clock that meal was the high point of the cruise.

Then we went on to the Steel Pier where we were completely fascinated by the miniature golf course. We played with a putter, and we played for a nickel a hole, one-tie-all-tie and a carry-over. On the fourth hole I sunk a long shot and the pot was mine unless Beau could tie it up. We all bent over to watch him putt, and when he missed, my elation was cut short by the head of his putter, which, swinging up in exasperation, caught me over the right eye. In two minutes my eye was closed, and in five I had a poached egg.

So we started back to the boat. By now it was blowing, blowing great guns right out of the northeast. Mario urged us to hurry. "Come on, gang," he said. "This doesn't look good." They had four lines out on the *Fat Cat* when we reached the dock, and she was pitching like a bronco. The tender was a mass of kindling wood tied to the painter. There was no getting aboard that night. She rolled and pitched until I was sure the mast would come out. We slept on the club porch under borrowed blankets, cold and morose. My cuckoo clock had returned. Draw the curtain. Draw the curtain.

Somehow we lived through the next two days until the wind blew itself out. Somehow we cleaned up the scrambled cockpit, somehow we tacked our way home three days late, noses peeling, out of sleep, hungry for home cooking.

Mort as always was a gentleman. I remember he put his hand on Mario's shoulder as we told him about the tender.

6

The Water Sports

IN midsummer the days ran together into those blissful variations on the Ocean and the Bay: tennis in the early morning with the clay court still damp, swimming before lunch, sailing, racing, tennis again, the enormous thirst when ice water from the cooler gave you a pain between the eyes, cherry jiggers or a marshmallow whip at Priest's, beach parties with roasting corn and sarsparilla, and the Hops on Saturday nights, when the college hatbands—Cottage, Ivy, St. Anthony, Psi U, and Zete — walked off with the older girls who had a smile for you during the week.

All too soon it was time for the Water Sports. They came on the Saturday before Labor Day, and jingo, where had the summer gone! On Friday, floats were towed up the Metedeconk River and anchored three hundred yards apart, and by Saturday noon the lane of open water between was lined by the entire output from the Yacht Club: the big cabin catboats, the *Romp* and *Pastime;* the Brewsters' fat sloop, the *Nan,* and Ruford Franklin's beauty; the sneak boxes and the Gloucester one-designs; the motorboats, the Sutphens' cabin cruiser and the Hydes' launch with its roomy cockpit — fifty or sixty assorted boats on each side, anchored deck to deck, and at the midpoint the Commodore's big black yawl, all rigged out in flags.

The small fry came first and the Tub Race was their climax. It took all the skill of the starter to ease the contestants into those round wooden washtubs, to line them up with toes touching the float — and make sure that no one sank before the start. At the crack of the pistol sixteen pairs of hands began thrashing the water. The overeager forged into the lead, filled up and submerged. You needed nice balance and a steady unsplashing rhythm to cover those fifty yards at a winning pace and not sink. A skinny guy with nervous energy had the edge.

Then came the swimming races with no one ever able to "crawl" as fast as Al Norris of Lawrenceville. Then the boats — the dinghies first, each cockleshell spurting along, oarlocks groaning, cutting a tangent, with the inevitable collision, and if Fortune laughed some contestant, in his haste, missing the water entirely. The canoes were more graceful, especially in the Singles when the undergraduate from Canada who had been taught by the Indians came through standing up. In the Doubles of course you always cheered for the most popular of the newlyweds, but somehow they could never steer a straight course. It was always a dogged middle-aged couple who wore them down and crossed the line first.

So the afternoon ran its course with plenty of refreshments — the basket lunch, the Shandygaff, and a special box of Huyler's Butterscotch Kisses for those too young to smoke. When each event was decided the winner swam, rowed, or paddled over to the Commodore's yawl to receive the tiny silver cup while everyone applauded with "Attaboy, Sam!"

As the shadows lengthened, the wind fell and now the lane of water was glassy and still. Now we were coming to the big event — the really tough one — the one that brought out the real fight in the contestants and the yelling partisanship of the spectators — the Tilting. From each end of the lane a canoe would appear, the paddler deep down in the stern showing only shoulders and head above the gunwale, the tilter standing feet wide apart and braced midships with his nine-foot bamboo pole, on the end of which was a fat swabber, canvas-covered. Warily they approached, each jockeying for the broadside, and then one paddler, seeing his opening, dug fast while his tilter thrust and lunged at the opponent, who was already beginning to teeter. You had to take it standing, and once those swabbers had soaked up enough water they really hit you. Every canoe had its cheering section and advice was free and loud, as the paddlers backed and feinted and dug for the quick turn that would catch a man vulnerable and off balance. These guys were our heroes, college juniors some of them; and when a swab slipped and the bamboo made a bloody gash along the arm, you could feel the shudder run through the boats. The semifinals got the blood up, and when the big boys came together in the face of the setting sun, it was something to see.

And then suddenly, the year before the war, surprisingly it was my turn, or rather Ed's. I was a little guy weighing ninety-four pounds in a wet bathing suit, and good only for the paddling. But Ed had a sunny courage (too good for the bullet which stopped him at Château-Thierry) with solid legs and a fine pair of arms. We entered just for the fun of it and in the preliminaries bowled over two boats, one of our own weight and one of the big shots who had grown just a little sluggish. My memory of the semifinals is dazed by the bedlam of shouts when Ed, who had stood up under a real pounding, suddenly caught our opponent in the chest, knocked him off his feet, and while their canoe was tipping from the fall, we closed in and rolled it over.

There was nothing uncertain about the finals. We were the underdog and we had the crowd with us. But the pole was a weary weight by this time, and my paddling was not as crisp as it had been. We circled our older opponents, made a pass, drew apart, and while I was backing to get a fairer position, they suddenly came piling in. "Turn!" Ed yelled. I tried, but too late. The swab caught Ed on the flank, then the seat, and lifted him, pole and all, into the Bay. It was so sudden the disappointment still rankles. I keep trying to do it over again hot nights before I drift to sleep.

7
The Colonel

A grandfather can be a very impressive figure and the grandfathers of my generation were invested with a special aura because of their part in the Civil War. We were the youngest to hear at first hand their stories of Shiloh, Chancellorsville and Gettysburg and shall be the last to remember how these veterans looked. To us they had the expectation of being obeyed, they had an oaklike hardihood and they had done things gallantly.

My grandfather, Charles Crook Suydam, was six foot two and of a size to command respect. He was "the Colonel" to everyone in town and the title was not complimentary; he had been in command of the Third New Jersey Cavalry at the age of twenty-seven. I knew that he had volunteered as a private in 1861, had been promoted and had served on the staff of General Keyes and then of General Pleasonton. But the old photographs posed by Brady before the open tents were as nothing compared to the legends told me by my aunts. He had had six horses shot under him, and one had rolled over on him crushing his leg and thigh. The doctor filled him with brandy and kept him on his feet, forcing him to pace back and forth on the ship bringing him home. The orderly steered him to the old house on Williamson Street and Grandfather entered, called "Lizzie, are you there?" and went down like a telephone pole.

In his old age, after Grandmother's death, he lived at the Mattano Club, and there on Sunday mornings I used to call for him. After Sunday School and Church I had a ravening hunger and on those special occasions when I was excused before the sermon and had time to loiter at the club Grandfather always recognized my symptoms. "What would you like?" he'd ask as I wiggled back into the deep, black leather armchair, and he'd push the little domed bell. Trouble was there really wasn't anything worth eating in the darn place. Never a piece of French pastry. I had to take what the members took. On a small table, mounted on a napkin, stood a large wedge of yellow cheese with a scoop spoon and some very dry crackers beside it. The steward brought me a tall glass of iced ginger ale and my treat began; the sharp cheese, dry crackers and dry bubbles made me sneeze but I was committed now and had to finish.

From where he was sitting in the bay window the Colonel could tell when the service at St. John's was over. Clamping those big hands of his solidly on each arm of the chair he'd heave himself erect. Lord, how big and starched he looked in his Prince Albert with the satin lapels and the Loyal Legion in his buttonhole. He'd take his silk hat and cane; I'd take his hand and we'd step out into the September sunlight for our walk up North Broad Street to Sunday dinner. People spoke to him: "Fine day,

Colonel. Good to see you looking so well!" and some of the respect they felt for him brushed off on me.

Sunday dinner with Grandfather was an occasion: the roast beef — he liked it rare — and roast potatoes; the Tiny Tims and creamed oyster plant had an extra flavor. After the dessert the old gentleman liked walnuts and a glass of port and I remember that once when Father was opening a fresh bottle the Colonel must have been nodding for when the cork came out with its small explosion he opened his eyes with a start: in that split second he told us he'd been back on the field at Gettysburg. But that is all he told us.

After dinner he didn't mind if I paged through the Leslie woodcuts of the war, the big volume on the floor and I at his knee. He never reminisced, just grunted the names of his great ones as he saw what I was looking at — "Burnside," "Phil Sheridan," "General Miles" — then the big head would sink down on his collar, the eyes close, and Mother would beckon me away.

Grandfather had known Lincoln — and with Grandmother, a bride then and lovely, he had dined at the White House; he had ridden in the triumphant review of the Army of the Potomac in that jubilant Washington of May, 1865, and like so many of his generation his career was then at its high point. I doubt if any subsequent command in civil life, not even the fractious years when he was one of Hetty Green's attorneys, ever called out of him as much as his charges against Jeb Stuart in the Valley. Six daughters but his only son dead . . . Lizzie gone, and a dwindling law practice . . . A front to keep up through a long anticlimax — but, of course, I knew none of this at the time.

I remember his great cavalry saber which I could barely lift, and the heavy horse pistol I was half afraid to draw from the holster; I remember his commission signed by Lincoln and his spurs on the top of the bookshelf. I remember the "4711" which he used on his handkerchiefs; his black broadcloth and immaculate starched shirts; and I remember his rebuking me on a visit to us for not having my toenails cut when I crept into his bed one Sunday morning before breakfast.

The stories about him were probably embellished in the retelling by the Colonel's six daughters, one of whom is my mother. The most exciting story was prompted by the miniature of Grandmother, painted on ivory. While inspecting pickets in the Shenandoah, the Colonel at full gallop was spotted by a sharpshooter; the horse was killed and he severely hurt. The wagon train in which he was sent to the rear was captured by Mosby's guerrillas: when Grandfather was being stripped of his belongings he asked if he couldn't keep his wife's picture, and the guerrilla leader had cracked the ivory with the butt of his pistol and tossed it over. But before the guerrillas could reach their own lines they in turn were surprised by Union cavalry under General Custer. So they were strung up, and this had all the switch and drama to dream about — and there was the miniature to prove it! Another story was about the Confederate shell in the library, a dud which had plowed into the ground beside Grandmother while she and the Colonel were riding close to the lines and evidently in view of a Rebel battery. I used to wonder what she was doing so close to the front. And did Lincoln really say to her, at the close of a White House reception: "And now, my dear, if you'll excuse me I think I'll put on my old slippers, my corns are very bad this evening"?

8

Christmas Eve

WHEN Taft was President a twelve-year-old living on an allowance of twenty-five cents a week had to begin saving up for Christmas in mid-October— that is, he did in a family like mine where there were brothers and sisters, father and mother, seven aunts and a beloved godmother, two favorite uncles, Uncle Joe and Uncle Harry, a grandfather, and three cousins, Harriet, Allen, and Puck, for all of whom presents had to be devised out of that twenty-five cents.

Devised is the word. For uncles you devised ash trays. For months you collected, uncoiled, and carefully pressed the best cigar bands that came into the house. These in their scarlet-golden glory were then pasted face up until they covered the entire underside of the glass tray. To give it a professional look the tray had a backing of green baize; and what a job it was to glue that on, evenly! Also, for the elders, were mottoes burned in wood with a red-hot poker, or better yet with a wood-burning needle if you knew somebody who owned one. "God Bless Our Home," "The Fear of the Lord is the Beginning of Wisdom," and one which I devised myself, "Sincerity, Simplicity, and Strength."

For cousins there were jigsaw puzzles made on borrowed time with the jigsaw which belonged to Freddie
who lived across the street. What you did was to take a
favorite picture like "Custer's Last Stand" in *Collier's,*
paste it with beautiful smoothness on the thin wood, and
then against the whiny little saw ("Don't push too hard,
Ted, or you'll bust it") cut out the little curlicue pieces
which would be packed in a Christmas box. For my best
girl, who collected stamps, I mounted a colorful assort-
ment of my duplicates in an unused diary for 1905. The
stationer would sell you old diaries for almost nothing.
With such devising, twenty-five cents a week could be
stretched just far enough to fill your list, and what you
couldn't make you went scouting for in the Five and
Ten. It seemed like a long time to have to save; but
while no one ever bothered to explain to us the innocent
pleasure of giving, we felt it just as much as we felt the
expectancy when the incoming presents from relatives in
Annapolis and St. Paul and New York arrived and were
shut away in the spare room. The mystery of what was
accumulating behind that closed door was something to
think about.

The children's service at St. John's on Christmas Eve
was the curtain raiser for the Great Day. The church was
festive and fragrant with greens, and in the wintry candle-
lit twilight the arches and vaulting seemed those of a
great cathedral and the altar shone with singular radi-
ance. Dr. Glazebrook led and we responded to those
magnificent words:

Christmas Eve

For unto us a child is born, unto us a son is given: and the government shall be upon his shoulder: and his name shall be called Wonderful, Counsellor, The Mighty God, The everlasting Father, The Prince of Peace . . .

A spirit like an electric current ran through me; and when later we rose to sing "O Little Town of Bethlehem" and the church was filled by the high young voices, it seemed that this was a moment of dedication. Hearing my mother's lovely soprano in the choir, I used to hold back my tears as we came to the last verse, and be ashamed lest my face should show it. Then came the gifts, the cornucopias for everyone, and the Testaments for those who had been perfect in attendance. Then came "Silent Night," and then the walk home on the crunching snow under the stars. If such faith and anticipation do not take the homeward path this Christmas Eve, our children will be the poorer for it.

I I
Books and Men

9
A Beginning Editor

ON a May afternoon in 1923 I sat in my living room in the Great Court of Trinity College, Cambridge, serving tea to my cousin, Mrs. Alice Duer Miller. My year of graduate study was almost at an end, and in another two months I should be back in New York looking for a job. Mrs. Miller was as charming a bluestocking as I have ever known; a Phi Beta Kappa and a mathematician, her serials had scored an enormous success in the *Saturday Evening Post,* her plays had done well, and she had a grace and attraction which melted men of any age. I had already melted and was on the point of being confidential. "Alice," I said, "I shall be looking for a job in three months, preferably in publishing. Got any suggestions?"

"Well," she said after a pause, "if I were your age, I can think of three men with whom it would be fun to work." Her use of that word *fun* made the whole prospect brighter. "The first," she said, "lives down on Long Island and is a little hard to get at. He is running a kind of secondhand magazine business, with his offices in a barn. He's had a slight tiff with his father, but I suspect he will eventually rejoin the family firm. His name is Nelson Doubleday.

"And then," she continued, "there is a man named

Harold Ross. He used to be one of the editors of *Stars and Stripes*. Now he's editing the *American Legion Monthly*, with offices on West 13th Street. You must be sure to see him. He is a rare one, and I believe he's raising money with which to start a new magazine. The third is Horace Liveright, a young speculator who has come up from Wall Street to put together the most astonishing list of books in less than five years' time. He would be fun, too."

When I got back to New York in early July I began pounding the pavements, and one of my first calls was on Harold Ross. He took time to see me, which is not always the case with a young job-seeker; and he was cordial. Yes, he said, he was leaving to start a magazine of his own, but he did not have any jobs whatever to offer, not until they began to work on the dummy four or five months from then. If I could afford to wait . . . But I couldn't, so there went my chance to begin with the *New Yorker*.

Later that week I applied to Horace Liveright in his ornately redecorated brownstone offices on West 48th Street (a shower bath behind one set of flamingo panels, a bar behind the other), and here, to my gratification, I learned that there was soon to be an opening. Their star salesman, Richard Simon, had given notice that in a matter of months he would be joining forces with a friend of his, Max Schuster, to start a firm of their own. Mr. Liveright was looking for someone to understudy Dick, and I was elected. Our interview took place on a Friday afternoon, and I went home for the week end with three advance copies, titles which I should be expected to sell the following week. I read them straight through. One was a comedy novel about the younger generation; the second was quite sexy; and the third was a collection of short biographies entitled *Strenuous Americans,* profiles of people like P. T. Barnum, Admiral Dewey and Frances E. Willard. I was going to be ready.

During my year in England I had had made up for myself a suit of brown English tweeds with a nap so long that the wool seemed to grow overnight. In this hairy suit I reported at Liveright's bright and early Monday morning carrying with me a tennis racquet and a small bag containing my sneakers and white flannels. I had a match late that afternoon at Forest Hills.

It was about 3:30 in the afternoon when Dick Simon suggested that I make my first assault on the book trade. "Let's take this book," he said, indicating *Strenuous Americans.* "We'll walk over to Scribner's and see what you can do. They ought to be good for fifty copies. The author, you know, teaches at Columbia. Have you got your order book? All right, let's go." I took along my racquet and tennis things, as it seemed natural to head for the courts on Long Island after my sale. We entered Scribner's and climbed to the mezzanine, I in my hot, hairy suit with the racquet and *Strenuous Americans.* There Dick presented me to George Whitworth, the head buyer: "George, I want you to meet Ted Weeks, one of our new salesmen."

"Hello," said Mr. Whitworth. "Well, what have you got there, a sexy book?"

"No," I said, putting down my tennis racquet and handing him the advance copy. "Biography."

"Have you read it?"

"Yes," I said.

"Like it?"

"No."

"Well," said Mr. Whitworth, "put us down for five copies and we'll do our best."

I solemnly entered the order in my new order book, picked up my tennis things and we departed. On the corner of Fifth Avenue, Dick, who is a very tall man, leaned over me. "Look, Ted," he said compassionately, "the next time you have a book like *Strenuous Americans* to sell I think I'd leave that tennis racquet at home . . ."

But I could learn, and I did. In the first place I learned to respect the authors who were being published under our imprint, many of whom I had never read before. Cousin Alice had said that it was an exciting list. This was in the fall of 1923, and here are some of the new books which Horace Liveright was about to offer the public: *The Wasteland,* a long poem by an unknown, T. S. Eliot; a collection of short stories, *In Our Time,* by another unknown, Ernest Hemingway; *Upstream,* by Ludwig Lewisohn; *The Emperor Jones* and the short plays of Eugene O'Neill; *The Story of Mankind* by Hendrick Willem Van Loon; *Arabia Deserta,* by C. M. Doughty; the novels of George Moore and Theodore Dreiser — all this in addition to *Flaming Youth* and *Black Oxen.* Of course I wasn't allowed to sell the big ones; they were handled by Julian Messner and Dick Simon. I drew the unknowns.

Tom Smith, the editor in chief of Boni & Liveright, was in Europe that summer and in his absence I was occasionally consulted on editorial matters. I arranged to have the manuscript of Van Loon's *Story of the Bible* read by two friends of mine, the Reverend Taggert Steele at Trinity's and Canon Vesey at St. John the Divine, and with their help I was able to warn Mr. Liveright that this book probably would not duplicate the success of Van Loon's *Story of Mankind*. Van Loon, who had finished the new manuscript in Utrecht, was a free thinker and a freer doubter: he was disagreeably skeptical about Christ's birth; ascribed the miracles to Christian Science or illusion; omitted the Sermon on the Mount and had nothing to say about the Resurrection. We tried to make up for some of these deficiencies by cable, but the tone of his treatment of the New Testament was so offensive that we were licked before we started.

I was being introduced to literary circles, particularly by my mentor, Frederick Lewis Allen, then the assistant editor of Harper's. He took me to lunch at the Coffee-House one day and sat me beside a man from out-of-town, a Bostonian by the name of M. A. DeWolfe Howe. He seemed a very kindly person and he stuttered as he asked about the work I was doing. I replied rather shortly, I am afraid, as I was all ears for the argument going on at the other end of the table where John Jay Chapman was storming away at Roman Catholicism, being baited and contradicted by his neighbor to the left, Heywood Broun.

To a novice they all seemed full of authority and fresh from Olympus.

But the main burden of my job was selling and I learned to bring more buoyancy to it. I made friends with the buyer, Ellen Ennis, at Lord and Taylor; I learned that the buyers at Macy's would seldom allow me more than a minute and a half in which to present each new title; I learned what to expect from Wanamaker's and how meager were the prospects in the Brooklyn department stores.

I scored an unexpected success with a book called *The Sacrificial Goat*. It was the first novel of a young, unestablished English writer, and it was supposed to be the clandestine love story of George Bernard Shaw. A modest quota had been set for it in the New York shops, yet here I was coming in with orders for fifties and hundreds, considerably ahead of what the boys had asked. I cannot remember how I had worked up my enthusiasm for that novel, but I had; and to clinch the deal I would quietly reassure the buyer that if he had a few copies left over after Christmas I was sure Mr. Liveright would be glad to take them back.

At Liveright's the reorders which came in each morning were spread out on a hall table for all to see. But as we passed Thanksgiving and came into the feverish weeks of Christmas buying it seemed that no one, literally no one, was reordering *The Sacrificial Goat*. Mr. Shaw did not explode in the expected libel suit, the reviews were brief and tepid, the advertising ceased, and there, as I made my rounds, stood those rows of accusing, unsold, immovable volumes on which I had expended so much good will. The buyers, too, began to look at them significantly, and I had a vision of all of these 'returns' being deducted from my pay check when they began to march home after Christmas. There would have to be, I knew, an accounting early in January; and even though Julian Messner, the head of our Sales Department, was the best-natured man in the world and very patient with me, I wasn't sure whether his temper would willingly absorb several hundred unsold *Goats*.

On my last pre-Christmas visit to Abraham & Straus in Brooklyn I found two or three salesmen ahead of me and so sat waiting my turn on the hard bench. In the interval I took out of my pocket a hand-written envelope bearing a Boston postmark which I had not had time to open at the office. The handwriting was distinguished but hard to follow, and it took me some moments to puzzle out that I was being asked to join the editorial staff of the *Atlantic Monthly* as an assistant, the second assistant, to Ellery Sedgwick, the editor in chief.

My father, who was a born New Yorker, was dead against it when I told him of the offer that night. "Don't touch it," he said emphatically when I showed him the letter. "Don't touch it. New York will always pay you better. And if you lose a job in Boston, you're out in the cold."

But I accepted, and on the second of January, 1924, presented myself at 8 Arlington Street. Mr. Sedgwick, who looked dark and rather Spanish, welcomed me and explained my duties. He led me into a large rear room with windows opening on a fire escape and there introduced me to Florence Converse, a bright-eyed, decisive little woman with the touch of a poet, from whom I was to learn much. We shared the room, our desks at an angle, and between them was a large old mahogany table on which stood three tin bread boxes. The first box was labeled TODAY, the center one YESTERDAY, and the third THE ABYSS OF TIME. Each day these boxes were stuffed with the newly opened manuscripts and each evening those which had been unassimilated were moved forward. Here it was I settled down to read, and so began my adult education.

10

Kipling Remembered

IT is the law of gravity in literature that those books we particularly value we press on others. This explains why Francis Thompson's exquisite essay on Shelley, the fourth of the slim volumes in the collected edition of his works, is invariably missing from the set. You wrote your name in it before you loaned it to your friend, then out into the dark night it went, never to return. And you can't remember the name of the pressee.

"You lucky dog," said my friend David McCord, the poet, "have you really got a first edition of *Seven Men?*" We were standing in front of the bookshelf holding my Max Beerbohm. "I loaned someone mine years ago." He reached up and pulled out the volume and there on the flyleaf in small script were the words, DAVID McCORD.

This law of gravitation works best among contemporaries. Inside the family, in the parent-child relationship, it is checked by the rebel belief that what appealed to our parents is too old, too dead, for us. *The Scottish Chiefs* was pressed on me by my godmother, and I did not yield. *Oliver Twist,* which I was encouraged to swallow at the age of twelve, did not reduce me to tears; I thought it a great bore, and those grimy, grotesque illustrations only added to my rejection.

But there was nothing forced about my love of Kipling. Mother read aloud to me the *Just So Stories,* the stories Kipling had written for his own son when he was a very small boy, and the words had beauty and a rhythm which once heard made you want to repeat:

I am going to the great gray-green, greasy Limpopo River, all set about with fever-trees, to find out what the crocodile has for dinner.

You had to repeat it, and you listened for it with delight every time the story was reread. "The Elephant's Child," the story of a young elephant who got his nose caught by a crocodile; "How the Camel Got His Hump," "How the Whale Got His Throat" — these stories were first spoken by father to son. When they were written, they were written to be read aloud. They are totally unexpected, and laughable, and full of wonder; and children like to hear them again and again.

I knew the *Just So Stories* by heart. As a small boy, I had a photographic memory, and on that memory Kipling's prose and illustrations made an impression that time did not erase. When I was old enough to recite at our public speaking at school, the teacher wanted me to memorize a poem by Robert Louis Stevenson, but I thought it was wet; I said I wanted to recite Kipling's story, "How the Whale Got His Throat," and I recited it there and then without a book.

After the *Just So Stories* came *The Jungle Book.* The

hero of the first story in *The Jungle Book* is Mowgli —
Mowgli the Frog, as the wolves called him, and he is
one of those children who will live forever. Mowgli is a
child of the jungle, who as a naked, brown baby of three,
strayed away from his home village in India, and wandered down a jungle path after dark. There the wolves
found him. But they didn't destroy him. Father Wolf, the
leader of the pack, carried Mowgli back into the cave
where Mother Wolf was nursing her new litter of cubs.
Suddenly the moonlight was blocked out of the mouth of
the cave by the great square head of Shere Khan, the
tiger, who demanded that the man cub be given to him.
But the wolves would not give him up. Who will ever
forget the warning of their leader, "Look — look well,
O Wolves!" So begins this wonderful story of a child
reared by a mother wolf, who learned to talk the animals'
language, and who always remembered that Shere Khan
was his enemy.

Mowgli learned to talk to the wolves and the tiger,
the jackals, the monkeys, and the birds. As he grew up
he became a power in the jungle even though he was a
boy of only nine or ten. And of course he did things that
every ten-year-old would dream of doing. He lived without fear, now in the treetops, now on the jungle trails;
he lived the free life — without homework, or measles,
or dancing school. And when at last the time came for
him to say farewell to the beasts of the jungle, and to return to his village, there was a lump in Mowgli's throat
as there certainly was in mine as I heard my mother read
the words describing his return to mankind. The village,

as I remember, put Mowgli in charge of their buffalo herd, and so it was, while watching those black-horned cattle, that he had his revenge on his old enemy, the tiger, Shere Khan.

There was another story in *The Jungle Book* which came very close to me — the story of Rikki-Tikki-Tavi, the mongoose. A mongoose is an animal about the size of a little cat, but rather like a weasel in his head and his habits. This particular mongoose, Rikki-Tikki-Tavi, had been adopted as a pet by an English family living in a big bungalow in India. The fact that the boy in the family was named "Teddy" — which was my nickname — and that he was my age made the story seem as if it might almost have happened to me. Rikki-Tikki-Tavi used to sleep on Teddy's pillow and come to breakfast riding on the boy's shoulder, and, like every mongoose, Rikki-Tikki had an instinctive enmity toward snakes. When one morning he encountered a cobra on the garden path leading to the bungalow, Rikki fought by instinct and for his family. I wonder how many boys — how many thousands of boys — must have longed as I did to have Rikki-Tikki-Tavi as a pet.

Then in the year 1908 my father bought for our library that beautiful set of Kipling's collected works in the brown binding with the white cartouche of the elephant on the cover, published by Scribner's. Of course the set wasn't complete then, as Kipling was still writing, and each time a new book of his appeared, the publisher would send us a copy in the uniform brown binding. Now I was old enough to read Kipling for myself. I read slowly, but these books, printed in a large clear type on soft linen paper, certainly were a joy. The first one that I read entirely to myself was *Stalky & Co.,* the story — a novel really — about three boys at a famous English boarding school. Their names are Stalky, McTurk (the Irish boy whom the others called "Turkey"), and the third boy who had the name of Beetle, so of course he didn't need a nickname. Kipling had a happy faculty for picking just the right names for his characters. These three friends formed a daring partnership, and naturally their antagonist was their teacher and housemaster, Mr. Prout.

This story begins in the summertime, and I remember that it seemed to me curious that English boys should be going to boarding school in summer. But that, I learned later, was the practice in some English schools. *Stalky & Co.* is a novel based on Kipling's own experiences, and very lonely experiences, as a schoolboy in England.

Kipling was born in India and as a child he spoke Hindustani more correctly than he spoke English. Then at the age of six this swarthy boy with lank straight hair, who might almost pass for a Hindu, was packed off to an English boarding school; during the long vacation he visited with an aunt. I am sure he must have been homesick for his parents and for India, and I imagine that with his strange looks and ways he would have been teased and bullied by the older boys. For five years young Rudyard Kipling swallowed the bitter pill of loneliness. Only at the very end of his schooling did he make friends and have the fun which are reflected in the book he wrote about that school, *Stalky & Co.*

Kipling came back to India at seventeen with rejoicing in his heart. After those lonely years in the damp, windy climate of England, after the cold schoolrooms and colder lodgings of London, he must have been overwhelmed on his return by the heat and dust, the color and crowding multifariousness of Indian life. It called out of him senses which he had almost forgotten he possessed. Heat, thirst, smell, fatigue, the moist pressure of woolen clothing, the relief of the fan, the benison of iced drinks — all these sensations aroused him after the long separation, and they made him what he is, the most sensuous master of the short story in the English language. He loved everything about India; it was the dreamland of his boyhood, and as a young journalist he began writing those imperishable stories about the British soldiers, and the civilians in India, and about the Indians themselves, and the animals and the jungle.

There were twenty-odd volumes in that set of Kipling, and I read them all, book after book, word for word, draught after draught. The love stories did not hold me: I was too young to know or care anything about the amorous temptations in a closely confined cantonment where there were few white women and many men. But *The Soldiers Three,* with their banter and courage, their recklessness and loyalty, were my musketeers. Fuzzy-Wuzzy made me feel the hazard of the Northwest Frontier, and I could picture the risk an English boy my own age would be in for, if he rode beyond the regimental limits as did Wee Willie Winkie (another story I learned by heart); I had never seen a polo game, but the fierceness of the riding,

[48]

the pounding hoofs, and the chock of the mallet were in my ears as I read that superb narrative of a polo pony, "The Maltese Cat"; I was in tears before I came to the end of *The Light That Failed;* and I felt I was the youngest subaltern present when, in that regimental mess with its blazing uniforms, the Toast to the Queen suddenly released that eerie and prophetic tale, "The Man Who Was."

At last I came to *Puck of Pook's Hill.* I was not always sure about the meaning of the oblique references in the poems, but I loved Puck's favorite exclamation, "By Oak, Ash, and Thorn!" and I caught the fragrance of the English countryside in sentences like these:

The pigeons pecked at the mortar in the chimney-stacks; the bees that had lived under the tiles since it was built filled the hot August air with their booming; and the smell of the box tree by the dairy-window mixed with the smell of earth after rain, bread after baking, and a trickle of wood smoke. . . .

In that great trilogy, "A Centurion of the Thirtieth," "On the Great Wall," and "The Winged Hats," I found in Parnesius my ideal hero; and without thinking much about it I assimilated what has come to be a lifelong respect for the fortitude, the discipline, and the hope where there is no ground for hope, that have made England what it is.

Puck of Pook's Hill was published in 1906 in Kipling's forty-second year; he had thirty long years ahead of him but little writing. It was deeply tragic that Kipling's only son should have been killed in action in the Irish Brigade early in the First World War, for with the loss of his boy the light went out of the life of one of our greatest writers. Grief froze up the stories and poems that might have come.

I I

The Suitor from Hannibal

I never saw him. I wish I had — the white suit, the shock of hair, the outspoken, pungent, cantankerous, lonely Mark Twain. Lonely, certainly, by the time I was a boy when I might have seen him and when he was living in solitary style in a rococo house in New York City tolerating his literary honors and mourning for Livy, who was dead. It was there my friend Ferris Greenslet, then the literary editor of the *Nation,* went to see him and Mark received him in bed, propped up with pillows, puffing at his pipe and brushing away the cinders which kept threatening to burn the blanket.

We take in Mark Twain through our pores — snatches of *Tom Sawyer,* read aloud in class, or perhaps even an episode memorized; then *The Prince and the Pauper;* then *Huckleberry Finn;* and then as we grow older *The Jumping Frog* and *A Connecticut Yankee in King Arthur's Court.* If we are fortunate, we have traveled a bit ourselves before we turn to the full enjoyment of *Innocents Abroad.*

Of all our missionaries abroad, Mark Twain was the shrewdest and the most picturesque. His physical traits, the shock of hair — it was russet then — the hawk nose and piercing eye, the white clothes and the Missouri drawl

[51]

which dominated lecture platforms and the table talk, were as unforgettable as his droll and corrosive wit.

The Civil War was just over and the country in need of amusement when in 1867 Mark started off on a pleasure cruise to Europe and the Holy Land. His expenses were being paid by a Sacramento newspaper, for which he was going to write articles about what he saw; and in his travels he expected to pick up the source material for some new lectures. What made the trip still more exciting for Mark Twain was that without intending to he fell in love. He fell in love with a picture, a picture of a girl, Olivia Langdon, from upstate New York. Her brother was a shipmate and the boy had with him a picture of his sister which Mark never forgot. He determined to meet her on his return from the cruise.

The map of the world has changed a good deal since Mark Twain set out on that tour which was to result in *Innocents Abroad,* but human nature is much the same as he found it. He was seeing the Old World for the first time, commenting with a salty, skeptical, unexpected humor which soon had all America laughing.

I think of his first impressions of Morocco. He saw Tangiers, visited the Moorish shops, and then he came up with his findings: "I would seriously recommend to the government of the United States," wrote Mark Twain, "that when a man commits a crime so heinous that the law provides no adequate punishment for it, we ought to make him consul-general to Tangiers."

But don't think that Mark Twain traveled simply as a scoffer. He was too shrewd a judge of the human animal

to see any part of the world through a single set of preju-
dices. He did indeed scoff where the foreigners had a
scoff coming to them, but he always balanced his criticism,
it seems to me, where some other value prevailed. Thus
when he saw a community of hovels, he wrote: "The
donkeys and the men, women, and children of a family,
all eat and sleep in the same room, and are unclean, are
ravaged by vermin, *and are truly happy."*

The beggars and the terrible poverty of the Near East
depressed him. "Oriental scenes look best in steel engrav-
ings," he wrote. "I cannot be imposed upon any more by
that picture of the Queen of Sheba visiting Solomon. I
shall say to myself, you look fine, Madame, but your feet
are not clean and you smell like a camel." The romantic
sons of the desert Mark likened to a party of "Digger Indians with very long spears in their hands, cavorting around
on old crowbait horses, and spearing imaginary enemies;
whooping, and fluttering their rags in the wind, and carrying on in every respect like a pack of hopeless lunatics."
As for their horses, Mark said he longed in all charity
to strip their harness off and let them fall to pieces.

Mark went through Egypt, Syria, Turkey and Greece;
he covered the Mediterranean, and at last in Venice he
did what we have all dreamed of doing. He went for a
trip in a gondola through the lovely canals of Venice.
Mark begins by describing his gondola, "that fairy boat in
which the princely cavaliers of the olden times were wont
to cleave the waters of the unlit canals, while the gay
gondolier in silken doublet touched his guitar and sang."
That was what Mark expected, but this is how he found

it: "An inky, rusty old canoe with a sable hearse-body clapped onto the middle of it," while the gondolier was a "mangy, barefooted guttersnipe." The gondolier, true to his calling, would indeed begin to sing. But after standing it for a while, Mark Twain warned him, "I am not going to have my sailing lacerated by any such caterwauling as that. . . . Another yelp and overboard you go."

The pleasant thing about Mark Twain's travel writing is its honesty of purpose: he never poses as an authority and some of his most skin-'em-alive writing is directed at the "old travelers" who have been there before. "I love to hear them prate and dribble and lie," says Mark Twain. "They always throw out a few feelers: they never cast themselves adrift till they have sounded every individual and know that he has not traveled. Then they open their throttle valves, and how they do brag and sneer and swell and soar. . . ."

Innocents Abroad quickly became a popular book; it established Mark Twain as a writer and he was soon under heavy demands in the Lyceum circuit. To read of the lecture hazards which Emerson and Mark Twain endured (Emerson carried his own blankets and often slept sitting up, there being no Pullman available) is to realize that we who travel the air today in Stratoliners which span the distance from Boston to Houston in nine hours stand less buffeting and get more sleep than our predecessors. In one of his love letters to Livy, Mark Twain gives this description of one lecture assignment in upstate New York:

The Suitor from Hannibal

I left Buffalo at 4 P.M. yesterday, & went to Dunkirk, & thence out to Fredonia by horse-car (3 miles), rattled my lecture through, took horse-car again & just caught 9:45 P.M. train bound east — sat up & smoked to Salamanca (12·30) stripped & went to bed in a sleeping car two hours & a half, & then got up & came ashore here at 3 o'clock this morning — & had a strong temptation to lie still an hour or two longer & go to Elmira. But I resisted it. By coming through in the night, I saved myself 2 hours extra travel.

I wonder how many celebrities, American or British, would take such punishment today.

Elmira was the home of Mark's fiancée, Olivia (Livy) Langdon, a sheltered, affectionate daughter of a wealthy family. It was inevitable that they would meet on Mark's return: his glimpse of her picture aboard ship had fixed that. Mark, now in his thirty-second year, was already well enough known as a humorist to rate a sixteen-hundred-dollar fee for a single talk in San Francisco. To Livy's parents he was a startling and rather unwelcome suitor, and to Livy — ten years his junior — a formidable but attractive wild man who was to be taken literally and to be tamed.

The courtship, with its surprising sobriety, its high moral tone — as when Livy made Sam read Henry Ward Beecher's sermons — and its lovely flashes when Sam's irrepressible humor breaks through, is at last disclosed for us in *The Love Letters of Mark Twain* — letters which were withheld from publication for nearly half a century and which derive additional warmth from the skillful matrix of their editor, Dixon Wecter. Mr. Wecter makes it clear that Sam was no misogynist; as steamboat pilot, gold prospector, and frontier journalist he had his sweethearts, but with a mother and a widowed sister to support, and with a stout sense of financial obligation, Sam couldn't afford to marry until his thirties. The editor also makes it clear that while Sam could be as funny as the devil on a lecture platform, he came from a curiously undemonstrative family. He never saw his own parents kiss each other. "Our village was not a kissing community," Sam wrote. So, of the two, once the love was recognized, it was Livy who was the more ardent.

Sam proposed and Livy turned him down. But in her letters she attempted to "civilize" him and her momentary success drew them closer together. He did read sermons to her; he took the pledge; he smoked less in her presence, and forswore profanity. It was all in the mood, and the mood and its aftermath live again in these letters. When Livy capitulated it was with an affection which really startled Sam: "She poured out her prodigal affections in kisses and caresses, and in a vocabulary of endearments whose profusion was always an astonishment to me. I was born *reserved* as to endearments of speech, and caresses, and hers broke upon me as the summer waves break upon Gibraltar."

But where did Sam Clemens come from, what was the boy like who grew up to be Mark Twain? Again we look to Dixon Wecter, that broad-shouldered, sunny Texan who was so happily engaged as the editor of the Mark

The Suitor from Hannibal

Twain estate when death cut short his research. Dixon was an invigorating biographer and a fearless critic; he had so much to do and I wish he had lived to do it.

Mr. Wecter's first task was to edit the largely unpublished love letters which Mark wrote to Livy; meantime he was familiarizing himself with the Mark Twain country: with Mrs. Wecter he made a river trip down the Mississippi with Mark's pilot book to help him pick up some of the old landmarks. He followed up every family clue in Florida and Hannibal, Missouri, the villages in which Mark grew up. All this in preparation for his projected biography of Sam Clemens, the first volume of which, *Sam Clemens of Hannibal,* he had completed before his tragic death in 1951.

Sam Clemens of Hannibal is an enchanting family portrait with young Sam in the foreground, and in the background Hannibal, "the white town drowsing in the sunshine of a summer morning." Here is the Kentucky-born Mrs. Clemens, who married her stern, upright spouse to spite a younger beau. She, like all her redheaded family, adored the color red; she liked games and dancing, constantly had premonitions, was completely mercurial and feminine; and who shall say how much of her gay chemistry formed the writer? Here is Sam's father, the Judge, the optimist and speculator, with his Virginian's pride and his flair for failure, going deeper into debt as he opens one after another in his endless chain of general stores. Here are Orion, the earnest, humorless older brother, who put the sure kiss of death on any venture he touched; the attractive older sisters, Margaret and Pamela; and Tom Blankenship, son of a drunkard, who lived across the street and who was the original of Huck Finn.

Hannibal itself emerges as a kind of Eden in the Genesis of the American dream; the open, roomy houses with their enormous fireplaces, and dogtrots and grapevine swings in the woods. The Christmas fare always included venison steaks, ducks, wild turkey, grouse, and quail. The Swiss Bell-Ringers provided their "chaste, novel and select musical entertainments" in the Second Presbyterian Church, but down in the taverns one heard the more popular tunes like "O, Susanna" and "Old Dan Tucker" mixed with the luscious political oratory of the day. There was an attempted elegance in the little-used parlors, and even the traveling circus had a clown who was "guaranteed 'a perfect gentleman.'"

The portrait of Sam is vigorous and understanding. Wecter shows us a charming, rip-snorting, tender-hearted boy, much less predictable than his vacuous older brother. We follow Sam from his birth in the little town of Florida in 1835 ("I increased the population by one per cent"), through his childhood; we see the Indian games on the edge of the dim woods with their hint of animal terror, and the family grief which Mark shared early when Margaret died of "bilious fever"; we see his schooling in the village of Florida and his sunny visits to the Quarles' Farm. We see Sam's naturalness with the Negroes; we see his stubborn apprenticeship under Orion on the *Journal* and his assertiveness as he began to write facetious fillers: "To prevent Dogs going mad in August: Cut their heads off in July." We hear the pledge which he gives his mother when in 1853 he quits Hannibal to find a printer's job in St. Louis — "I do solemnly swear that I will not throw a card or drink a drop of liquor while I am gone." A book like this is a delightful tonic to the American spirit. Its warmth, its honesty, its exuberance are balm to the mind. The boy comes back and we wish we had known him.

12

Cockaigne

IN writings of the sea H. M. Tomlinson has been my navigator since my junior year in college. That spring a girl I was courting gave me a copy of his first volume of essays, *Old Junk*. The prose with its light, its power and mystery, and the almost Elizabethan choice of words had such an effect on me that I took the slim volume with me the following summer when I worked my way over to Scotland on a cattle boat. We were nine days out from Montreal and I was starved and arm-weary from watering and feeding those thirsty steers when on the last morning I finished my chores and went forward to the prow of the ship. I stood there watching the bow cleave its way through the olive dawn, watching the seascape turn from dull green to bronze, and then, far in the distance, the first rays of sunlight, as in a huge Victorian canvas, began to pick out the grazing sheep on the Scottish uplands, the flushed entrance to the Clyde and the lacework of masts and docks upriver. We passed a bell buoy, mournfully sounding, and I, half shivering in the cold, suddenly felt admitted to that mysterious marine world which Tomlinson has made his own.

Later I read his masterpiece *The Sea and the Jungle*,

which casts something of the same spell as *Lord Jim* (Conrad, I knew, was one of Tomlinson's heroes); after that I made vicarious excursions in his *London River*. Then when Britain stood alone in 1940, Tomlinson's essays, like Churchill's speeches, proclaimed the valiance of a great people in tones and words which had almost been forgotten in the 1930's, and I was proud to print them in the *Atlantic*. We had become friends-by-letter by now, and so when I flew to London in the summer of 1943 it was my luck to have "Tommy" call for me at the Savoy and pilot me to the London docks. His lined face — he was in his mid-seventies — was animated by his characteristic eagerness and compassion, and his creaking Cockney voice with its unsuspected music fitted the man. A young woman in the WVS uniform drove us into the neighborhood of the Liverpool Docks. As we walked Tomlinson began to tell me the story of those Docks and of the longshoremen who kept them working under the worst of the blitz.

He began with a tribute to the retired sea captains — Captain David Bone in his middle seventies was only one of many — who came back from permanent shore leave to resume command in the convoys. Somehow, he said, they seemed to rejuvenate in uniform.

He spoke of the Ship Exchange, that roomful of forty men at a spot marked "X," who directed each convoy as it came within forty hours of the Isle, splitting it so as to miss the raiders, berthing it in big ports and little all along the coast, and having trains on the sidings as the ships came in, so that no cargoes were lost to weather or bombs.

We approached the river down narrow streets along

[61]

which the dockworkers once lived. Those endless rows of dingy homes were now crippled or in rubble, and through the cavities one caught glimpses of the Thames.

Tomlinson was looking for something. "I don't know whether it has survived," he said. "I can't believe it has come through the blitz." But it had. A little old pub which Dickens used to visit. "That's it! My father used to come here when I was a boy." The neat, burnished taproom was still being used, though no one was in it when we entered. I was led farther along the corridor and out upon a little balcony hanging right over the water. "Now look," said my guide. "There is Limehouse Reach. And this is where Whistler made his etchings." The tide was low, below us lay the barges, and the pictures came back like echoes. Only the big ships were missing.

As we resumed our walk, Tommy told me the story of how one night at the height of the blitz freighters loaded with high explosive were piloted by a famous harbor master coolly and accurately through the narrow London locks while sparks hissed into the water from the falling walls and the Isle of Dogs went up in flames. "He was taking them down-river out of reach of destruction and any moment might have been his last."

So speaking, he guided me through the streets of his childhood, past the ruined chapel in which he and his wife had been married, through the St. Catherine Docks and from quay to quay until we reached the inner locks. Tanks with the Maple Leaf insignia of Canada were beetling off a transport, and to our left a landing barge, spick in its blue paint and with its new crew aboard, was making stealthily for the open river. We stood evidently where civilians were conspicuous, for there came running feet and a stern voice saying, "Here now, have you a camera?" It was the harbor master, the old hero, in his shiny, serge uniform and breast of old ribbons, but his grimness relaxed when he recognized Tomlinson. They had grown up on those docks, fished from them together in the 1880's. Navy reticence being what it is I should never have heard their banter about Cockaigne unless I had been in Tommy's keeping.

The great gates of St. Catherine's Dock, the little round guardhouse, and such fragments of the warehouses as were still standing were of old, yellow brick built when Napoleon was a threat. In the broad cobblestone yard cats were sunning. "Are those cats still on rations?" Tomlinson asked an inspector. "Yes, sir, they keep down the rats."

To our right was a large inlet, a quadrangle of bare quays into which ships passed, through a narrow lock. "Look there," said Tomlinson, and he pointed to the quadrangle. "The American clippers used to dock there. On those quays were once three tiers of warehouses with arcades and pillars. The ships lay along the walls beside the big arcades, with the masts above the top — and it was a sight. I've seen so many ships there you could walk from deck to deck, half across the water. Their bowsprits overhead were like the boughs of trees." Now there was not a ship in sight. "Gone — it's all gone," said Tomlinson.

We stepped out of the hot sunlight and descended into the cool chambers of the Crescent Wine Vaults, where, with our candles on the yard-long sticks, we poked for a little among the twenty acres of monastic tomb in which still lie sleeping tuns of old Madeira and Sherry, soft and mossy to touch, with the sugary stalagmites at the bottom to show the half-century of aging. "A man could get lost down there," said the old caretaker. "Forty miles of tracks. That's why we give you a candle — can tell you're missing if you don't return the stick."

So on to the Spice Docks and the Ivory Docks, and then down to the quay where a rusty freighter was unloading Demerara sugar. "Below her," Tomlinson pointed, "was where the *Torrens* moored — I have seen her here, when Conrad was her mate. . . . But you can't see it as I see it," he added. "All you can see is what's left." And glancing at his face, which had closed, I knew I couldn't. For what he was seeing was a small boy there, with his father, and the ships and the barges and the bustle, and the bowsprits and broad-beamed men in dark blue. They were all gone, not even the landmarks left.

I think we forget what strength there is in age. We are so used to having men burn themselves out, we forget the light that can be rekindled by crisis. Men of Tomlinson's generation have seen two worlds go by the board, and their loss should be double ours. But while there is still hope for a third, they have no time for repining. They are not watching from the city walls; they are working with all the strength of their experience and eloquence to preserve what must not be lost again.

It was Tommy who wrote me of H. G. Wells's death in 1946. Yes, I had read the news in the paper but here was a contemporary who had known him and grieved. Wells, too, was a Cockney trained (and imprisoned) as a draper's apprentice and yet self-educated with such prodigious energy that he broke the fetters and rose to be a brilliant, fearless and prophetic novelist. With Masefield, Conrad, Shaw, Galsworthy, and Bennett, he wrote for the Anglo-American world: his books were as much at home on our side of the water as in England. As Kipling spoke for the Empire and in stories like *The Man Who Was* foreshadowed the Churchillian suspicion of Russia, so Wells spoke for Britain in the calm before the storm. Both Kipling and Wells looked down the muzzle of the gun, knowing it was loaded, but it was Wells who, in books we refused to take seriously, foresaw the death-dealing of the two world wars and who imagined national suicide carried to its irresistible conclusion.

Here was what Tomlinson said of him:

DEAR TED:

I took your letter, all so friendly, to Bideford in Devon, to read again, and to answer from there; but that land of Amyas Leigh and Salvation Yeo (I suppose you have read Kingsley's *Westward Ho!*) is so still and sleepy a place, and yet with a light of so bright a quality, as if it retained the virtue of genesis and innocence, that I did no writing at all. (Yes, one piece — a tribute in memory of H. G. Wells for the Society of Authors magazine, for he was an old friend of mine as well as a great man.) His going, which was expected, left an awful emptiness of horizon; so I was left to stare at some familiar scenes I have put into *Old Junk* and *Gifts of Fortune,* and brood on the past, and on change, and progress. The light of Bideford Bay is just as it was before

Books and Men

America was discovered, or the Armada fought; but I am older; and Wells is dead.

My wife was with me. We spent our honeymoon at Appledore, below Bideford, at the mouth of the Torridge, and once more we sat on the sternboard of the *Mona* (that craft sails in *Old Junk*) with Yeo himself handling the mainsheet, as he did over forty years ago; and the lapping of the water under her prow was as if I could hear the past. Nevertheless, there the rusting craft of the Normandy landings were lying up, on the sands of a falling tide, and Yeo once removed his pipe to remark that if "They" don't renounce the atomic bomb, "They" will use it again. "The only way to get rid of the next war," he said, through his pipe, which he wears habitually, "is to jettison the means to make it." He always was a wise old bird.

I wish you had been with us. I'd have shown you something for your eye. Not that I haven't wished also that I had been with you and your son catching trout at Beverly, and by the Penobscot with you and David McCord (my love to him, too). Though how America will ever be seen again with these eyes, with prices and visas what they are, is past thinking of, I'm afraid. The greater the speed and the facilities of travel in this Age of Science, the less the poor can move about. Another victory in a war for freedom and we shall all be slaves, as a Frenchman recently remarked.

And yet there is much I want to say and to ask of you. Like others here — I mean writers — I am completely puzzled by contemporary literary opinion in America. I can't make out why this and that is admired on your side; and why what once was the accepted standard — here and with you — is now, apparently, in the everlasting discard. I think most American readers must be unconscious that anything has happened, yet that their standard has ceased to be anything like the one we still hold is causing us as much perplexity as Russia's view of democracy. I could give you instances (gathered mainly from the reviews and quotations in a famous American monthly, but not the *Atlantic*) though I will not. Something, anyhow, has happened on your side to the art of writing, and to the values that one ought to look for in a book; and I am curious, and want to hear you speak about it. I say, *hear* you.

Have you noticed that no contemporary Britisher now sells his book on your side, except one name or two, or three or so? Not that this matters much to me personally, except that I had been hoping that the last time I was in Boston was not the last time. Still, it does matter to English letters. It does matter to our cultural relationships; we ought not, in art, to puzzle each other. After all, Whitman did not puzzle London when he yawped. There was even rejoicing over here. Is it the new era of Hollywood and bulk productions? Is that it? Once again the machines, the technologists, and the promoters, this time to the undoing of art? Well, I suppose we must expect it. Machines before manners!

I read this week a long inquisitive interview with a man, now on a visit to London, who, it appears, bosses the censorship of films in California — an unofficial censorship, except that the producers themselves are its employers; and his views of what's what, and of virtue, and the real right thing in letters, had to be read to be believed. Even so, I might have supposed the interviewer was not quite just to that man; but his portrait went with the printed matter. That convinced me. There *was* such a man, and such opinions of supreme authority where writing is concerned. O God, O Nature! There it is. I don't like this New Age. In fact, I hate it. If it isn't the devil's

work, then it isn't anything like the Divine Purpose I have
innocently accepted as vital to our direction in all we do. Bless
you!

TOMMY

Is it true then that our worlds are growing apart? Here
is one way to test the question. During the First World
War approximately 30 per cent of the *Atlantic's* content
came from British writers and there were issues in which
they outnumbered the American contributors. But in the
years 1940–1945 our contributions from Britain seldom
ran higher than 15 per cent of our total. This decline in
our intercourse was a direct result of the Island's exposure:
the intensity of war work and the hammer blows of the
Luftwaffe left little time or place for creative writing. Men
too old for the uniform could find no sanctuary comparable to that which enabled, which even stimulated, Galsworthy, Wells and Co. to do their best from 1914 to 1918.
The sharp decline in the quality and number of British
manuscripts was a direct result of Göring's censorship.

Where there was so much fortitude, there was bound to
be some good writing, however sparse: Laurence Binyon's
poems, Tomlinson's and Bertrand Russell's essays, and
Churchill's speeches; Rebecca West's *Black Lamb and
Grey Falcon;* Toynbee's history; the poems and criticism of
T. S. Eliot; the essays of Cyril Connolly; the novels of
Arthur Koestler and Howard Spring; the poems of Dylan
Thomas and Dame Edith Sitwell; the monumental auto-
biography of Sir Osbert Sitwell; and *Brideshead Revisited*
by Evelyn Waugh.

[68]

Cockaigne

To people of less stamina this would have been a time of silent despair. I recall a passage in a letter from Sir Osbert written in 1944 when he was midway in his big work:

> I find it a heartbreaking time at the moment; a people with no future throwing away their past. But when things look like that it generally means the English are, contrary to what appears possible, going to do something big. So I continue to hope. I am a confirmed lover of lost causes. I begin to love all the people and things against which I've railed and roared for thirty years; such as Churchill, the Empire, and the military circles.

That recovery which Sir Osbert prophesied has come to pass. Contemporary English literature has recovered from the paralysis of the war. Nor should we overlook the feeling of reciprocity which began to flow across the Atlantic while the struggle was on. Books were a very real part of Lend-Lease to Britain, and American authors — Hemingway, Marquand, Steinbeck, Robert Frost, Faulkner — brought a fresh American quality to a hungry market. A novel like *For Whom the Bell Tolls* could not be kept in print; there was not enough paper to satisfy the demand. By 1943, 37 per cent of the new books read in Great Britain came from this side of the Atlantic. This had never been so before. And it continues.

13
Thackeray in America

IN late October, 1852, a good-natured British lion and his secretary were inbound to Boston aboard the passenger ship *Canada*. It was his first trip to the New World and he was coming over to lecture, urged to do so by James T. Fields, the Boston publisher, and wisely advised during the passage by James Russell Lowell, who was soon to be the first editor of the *Atlantic*. The lion stood six feet four, was broad-shouldered, with hair prematurely silver. He was Dickens's only rival, and his latest novel, *Henry Esmond,* would appear in London during his absence.

The crossing had been rough. The passengers had spent thirteen days "in that horrid little cabin below where we are tumbling and rolling and bumping and creaking in the roaring black midnight," and Thackeray was a relieved and hungry man when at last he reached the Tremont House, where rooms had been engaged for him. Fields had already ordered the dinner and invited a few friends, and remembering Thackeray's curiosity about American oysters, had taken care to procure the largest specimens available. Six Falstaffian bivalves were served to him in their shells. "How shall I do it?" asked Thackeray with a look of anguish. He was told. "Opening his mouth very wide," wrote Fields, "he struggled for a moment, and then all was over. I shall never forget the comic look of despair he cast upon the other five over-occupied shells. I broke the perfect stillness by asking him how he felt. 'Profoundly grateful,' he gasped, 'and as if I had swallowed a little baby!'"

Although people did not turn out with flags and drums to receive him, as they had Dickens a few years earlier, they did come, and in droves, to hear Thackeray lecture. He had prepared a series of six talks on "English Humorists of the Last Century," and when he needed a seventh, as he did before the tour closed, he dictated it in the course of a single day, lying in bed, chain-smoking and dictating to his secretary from breakfast until the dinner gong rang. His talks were amusing, his tenor voice carried well, and his accent was fascinating. Although he might down canvasback ducks and no little claret before mounting the platform, he never forgot for a moment that he was here to entertain. He needed the dollars, for his daughters and for his wife, who had long since been in a sanatorium. His fee was about five times larger than the going rate of our native talent. He expected the tour to net him close to twenty thousand dollars (which Baring's were to invest for him at 8 per cent in America), but when Providence turned out only 500 strong, half filling the auditorium, he was quick to return half the promised amount. "Nobody must lose money by me in America," he wrote, "where I have had such a welcome and hospitality."

To judge from the comments, it was the charm of what he said, even more than the substance, which brought down the house. William Cullen Bryant, covering the first lecture, on Swift, for the New York *Evening Post,* was impressed by Thackeray's gigantic size and by the fact that he looked so old; he praised the enunciation and the "utter absence of affectation of any kind" and the lecture itself as a "work of art." Yet he had little respect for Thackeray's summing up of the Dean's character, and other New Yorkers, notably Henry James the elder, were even more severe. "Thackeray," James said, "could not see beyond his eyes, and has no ideas, and merely is a sounding-board against which his experiences thump and resound: he is the merest boy." I gather that he was at his best in what he calls the "very good fogyfied literary society" of Boston, where with congenial men like Dana, Fields, Longfellow, and Lowell he would fall into that easy chat of which he was master. As Prescott the historian wrote of him: "I do not think he made much impression as a critic. But the Thackeray vein is rich in what is better than criticism."

And how did he find us? He came to us not as so many Englishmen have, with pride that only fortifies itself, but open and ready for new impressions.

"Broadway," he wrote, "is miles upon miles long, a rush of life such as I never have seen . . . houses are always being torn down and built up again . . . the rush and restlessness please me, and I like (for a little) the dash of the stream." "They begin without a dollar and make fortunes in 5 years . . . the pace is awful. No man lives in his father's house. . . ." "In 50 years the population will treble that of Britain. . . ." "Here is the future: here is the great English empire to be when the Gauls and Cossacks may have trampled out our old freedom. . . . Lord Lord I am going away presently a thousand miles to give a few lectures: a thousand miles is as nothing here: there are thousands and thousands beyond Cincinnati; and plenty and liberty for every man for hundreds of years yet to come. I almost feel young again as I drink up this young air."

I have been quoting copiously from *The Letters and Private Papers of William Makepeace Thackeray,* so skillfully edited by Gordon N. Ray. One enters and is absorbed by the intimacy, the many-peopled activity of these pages in which the manly, pensive, bantering voice of Thackeray awakens the characteristic response from "Old Fitz," from Fields, from his differing and adoring mother in Paris, from his two sprightly daughters, and from those women to whom he turned in his loneliness. "I can't live without the tenderness of some woman," he wrote to Mrs. Brookfield even as he knew that he was breaking with her; he felt that he was too old and spent, past his prime (at forty-two!), too old for the American Beatrix, Sally Baxter, whom he had found in New York and was falling in love with. What emerges from the reticence of these later letters, what identifies us so touchingly with the man, is Thackeray's feeling of insecurity at the thought of oncoming death, his urgency to make money now, and quickly, for his children and demented wife, before he goes, and his realization that he is spending himself prodigiously. When vitality surges up in him, he feels an incentive for public life, for Parliament, perhaps; and when he is down, he confesses his fading interest in literature. ". . . But not novels, nor lectures, nor fun, any more. I don't seem to care about these any more, or for praise, or for abuse, or for reputation of that kind. That literary play is played out, and the puppets going to be locked up for good and all."

It was Thackeray's mother who bade him "journalize" his doings and thanks to that habit we have this unsparing self-portrait: his gaiety, his love of wine and the theater, his aspiration to draw, his passion for gambling, his many rebuffs before success. I feel that I have come to know Thackeray, and not only Thackeray but his inner circle here, in London, and in Paris. And I feel that we owe Mr. Ray immeasurable gratitude for the fair-mindedness, the enormous patience and sympathy, and the self-effacing scholarship which have made these four volumes as impeccable as they are alive.

14
A Boston Publisher:
Alfred R. McIntyre

HE was slender, remarkably erect and wiry; you registered these impressions as you responded to his smile. It was the wide smile of a strong jaw, a jaw which could set with a Scottish tenacity that was not stubbornness. He was diffident, painfully so; yet it was his daily necessity to screw up his courage and walk out of his shyness to be his forthright self. The eyes were level and inquiring; as he came to meet you — and you, an author, or editor, or fellow publisher — he was readying himself for your particular problem. I never knew him to generalize, which is so often the easy way to evade; he had no evasion in him. I remember once talking to a young author who had come on to Boston after trying to place his work in New York. The unhappy man, recounting his failure, remarked, "When I told those publishers in New York how long my novel was and the problems I was struggling with in it, why they just turned and looked out the window." Alfred McIntyre never looked out the window; he looked at you.

The eyes, the smile, and the jaw — and as you came to know him, you watched his hands. They were thin-fingered and at times more expressive than his words. His hands would rise instinctively from the desk as his eyes lit up to a new possibility. I remember the sweep of his right hand as if to wipe a slate clean when with, "Forget it. You can't always be right" — he'd dismiss a problem we had been worrying at; and then there was another gesture when he'd raise his hands breast-high and suddenly drop them to the table in honest doubt — he didn't know the answer, we had made our investment and only time would tell. Because he was inherently shy, he was not given much to handshaking or shoulder-patting. But his hands talked.

I have stressed his tenacity. It is one of those rare qualities in publishing, the quality of holding onto an author and continuing to believe in him (and pay him his advance royalties) even if, year after year, the public turns a cold shoulder to his new books.

In 1933 Alfred began publishing a new English novelist by the name of C. S. Forester. He believed in this man Forester. He believed that he was a fine storyteller. He published each new novel of Mr. Forester's; first came a book called *The Gun,* followed by *The Peacemaker* and *The African Queen;* then a wonderfully ironic novel of the First World War, called *The General.* But American readers would have none of them — just weren't interested. Then Mr. Forester wrote a new book about a British sea captain at the time of Lord Nelson, a plucky, diffident officer by the name of Captain Horatio Hornblower; *Beat to Quarters* appeared in 1937, and all of a sudden the American public woke up. Everybody began talking about the Hornblower books. They were serialized, chosen by book clubs, they headed the best-seller list. People even went back and discovered how good were the earlier novels by Mr. Forester. Of course, they would never know with what tenacity Alfred McIntyre had believed in those early books when nobody would buy them.

Mr. McIntyre took over the publishing of Evelyn Waugh's novels in this country at a time when his early books were virtually unread. For all his Yankee reserve, he was swept off his feet when first he read *Brideshead Revisited*. He felt he had a good novel here, one which would be given a wide reading in this country, and he was shocked when, in the course of getting it ready for print, word reached him that the book had not even been recommended by the first readers of the Book-of-the-Month Club. Alfred was greatly troubled and in a last appeal sent a set of galley proofs to John Marquand with a personal note urging him to read it. Marquand in turn was captivated. He called the novel to the attention of the other judges, it was rated an A book, and was finally selected. Here again McIntyre's tenacious belief in Waugh's talent finally aroused American readers to a belated appreciation of this skillful English satirist.

Year after year at our sales conferences I have heard him identify the virtues of new books, many of them by authors then unknown. I can still catch the emphasis of his voice and the terse phrases with which he recommended those authors to the salesmen.

With his tenacity went a friendliness, a friendliness deep and abiding despite his starched New England appearance at his office at 34 Beacon Street. His friendship with John Marquand is a perfect example. With his serials and his short stories, particularly his Mr. Moto stories, Mr. Marquand had risen to be one of the most popular and highest paid writers in the magazine field. His books had never attracted the reading public, but Marquand, who had begun as a novelist, went on thinking in terms of books — and in 1935, he began to experiment with what was for him a new medium. He wanted to puncture the pompous ancestor worship which afflicted some old Bostonians. He wanted to accentuate the changes in American living and to satirize his native state, Massachusetts, which he knew so well. For months he worked at this experiment and when the book was about half done, he showed it with honest misgivings to an agent in New York. The report he got back was flatly discouraging.

Marquand was deeply troubled and in his dilemma he wrote to his publisher, who was also his friend, Alfred McIntyre. I am going to quote from that letter, and as you read it, please remember that the manuscript Mr. Marquand is talking about is *The Late George Apley*.

The last two months I have been working on a thing which I have often played with in the back of my mind, a satire on the life and letters of a Bostonian. I have now done some thirty or forty thousand words on it, and the other day showed it to a friend whose literary judgment I greatly respect, who feels it is a great pity for me to waste my time in going ahead with it. I suppose the most damning thing that can be said about the whole business is that I, personally, have enjoyed writing it, and think it is amusing, and think that it is a fairly accurate satire on Boston life. I certainly don't want to go ahead with the thing, however, if you don't think it holds any promise, and is not any good. Besides this, I do not, for purely artistic reasons, feel that the thing can be helped by any great changes such as injecting more plot, or by making the satire more marked. In other words, if it is not any good as it stands, I think I had better ditch it and turn my attention to something else. As this is the first time in a good many years that I have been in a position to write something which I really wanted to write, I naturally feel bad about it. I know you will tell me frankly just how it strikes you, and its fate rests largely in your hands. Tell me quickly.

McIntyre did tell him quickly. He said, "John, I personally think it is swell. I can't tell you whether it will sell more than 2000 copies — it may be too highly specialized. But by all means, go ahead with it!" And again his judgment was amply vindicated. Small wonder that his authors were so devoted to him. Later, as the dedication for his novel *So Little Time,* John Marquand wrote these affectionate words:

To Alfred McIntyre. In memory of all the trips we have taken together over the rough road of fiction.

I remember the true story of the famous publisher who in the days when Boston had a monopoly of our best writers was scolded by his wife for bringing so many of his writers home for meals. "Well, my dear," remonstrated the publisher, "I may bring them home for lunch, but I shall never force them on you for dinner." From what I have said you will see that publishing has changed. A good publisher today is often the closest friend that an author

[79]

has. The one fights for the other and there is reciprocity in their friendship.

Alfred McIntyre was the hardest fighter I have ever known in the book trade. He was a good trader and he loved to trade. But once the agreement was made, he stood by his promise to the full measure of his words and without deviation. He fought to see that the bookseller was not squeezed to the wall by the ever-growing book clubs and by the wholesalers, and this, of course, involved an adjustment of discounts which would be fair to the one-man, undercapitalized bookshops which in the sum are so important. He fought against the skeletonizing and digesting of books: he would not give the American public the illusion that a 90,000 word novel which had taken ten months to write could honestly be cut to 25,000 words and sold on a platter in a twenty-five-cent magazine — that, he said, was grossly unfair to the author and to the reader. He fought against those department stores which wanted to slash the publishers' price and use books as "loss leaders" — as bait to get new customers into the store. As early as 1927, he began fighting just as vigorously against the high prices and the overproduction which were always tempting the gamblers in publishing. "Fewer and Better Books" was the slogan he wrote and inserted in Little, Brown's colophon on the one hundredth anniversary of the firm. In his daily practice, which was also his philosophy, he worked for the dignity of the book and for the protection of the author and for the fair profit of those who sell books.

For ten years while I was editing *Atlantic* books, I was

in almost daily contact with him. The *Atlantic* had published exactly one novel in the decade preceding, and now I was being given my chance to enlarge the harvest. With the magazine to draw from and prize contests to encourage the new writer, the list grew from fifteen to twenty to twenty-five new books a year. It was an exciting build-up, and through it all Alfred McIntyre was my Supreme Court.

He had the most astonishing grasp of detail. We were struggling together once for the right title for a new novel by Walter Edmonds, a novel describing the fortitude and misery of the colonists in the Mohawk Valley at the time of the American Revolution. Walter as I remember had called his story *A Starving Wilderness,* which was not exactly an inviting title for the Depression. Alfred, as he fingered through the manuscript, said, "These people lived in the Mohawk Valley. 'Mohawk' is a good word." Pause. "How did the news of the Revolution first reach them?" "Why," I said, "I guess it was when they first heard the drums of the Continentals." "Drums," he said, *"Drums on the Mohawk.* No, you need more movement — *Drums Along the Mohawk."* And there was the title.

I remember that when *Good-bye, Mr. Chips* was first offered to us, James Hilton was willing to sell the book outright for a small sum (enough cash to provide him with a short holiday in Switzerland!), and that Alfred cabled him that any outright sale was against his best interests, sent him the money he needed as an advance and with it a good contract.

[81]

He read his competitors' books just as carefully as his own. I remember a famous elephantine novel which had been published by one of our greatest rivals and chosen by the Book-of-the-Month Club. Alfred procured an advance copy and began reading its more than thousand pages. Then, being in the neighborhood, he went in to see the publishers of the book. "Quite a book you've got there," he said to the publisher. "Have you read it?" "Well, no, actually I haven't," said the publisher. "but everyone here who has is crazy about it." "Better read it," said Alfred in tones reminiscent of Cal Coolidge. "Take a look at Page 158!"

Knowing Alfred's integrity, the publisher went into high gear. And there on the page Alfred had spotted was a paragraph so offensive that it would have seriously hurt the book's sale, a paragraph, incidentally, which had slipped by the notice of five judges of the Book-of-the-Month Club and the entire editorial staff of the firm. The first edition was recalled; the page revised.

You can see how things like that endeared him not only to his own authors but to his competitors. With all of his diffidence, he was easily one of the best-beloved publishers Boston has ever produced. Cocktails he enjoyed as much as any man; but cocktail parties, which are an occupational risk in publishing, he loathed with the shyness of a man who cannot remember names. This shyness, curiously enough, he overcame at literary dinners. I remember his presiding at the full-dress banquet which celebrated Little, Brown's Centennial; and I remember the spontaneous ovation, a complete surprise to him, which the New York publishers gave him as they rose to their feet. I see him at the head of the table at his annual stockholders' dinners — the mellow light, and the affection and intimacy with which he drew the men together.

At the war's end, Dr. Alice Hamilton, one of the wisest women in industrial medicine, was talking to me about the physical exhaustion of the war. "Men of forty-five to sixty are coming out of it far more tired than they realize," she said. "Yet they are the very men whose strength and experience we most need. I hope we can keep enough of them alive."

In the years which intervened the problem of publishing, which was never secure on more than a narrow margin, became increasingly difficult. The high cost of paper, of labor and of composition led us into a vicious circle. The cost of producing a book has more than doubled since 1939 and in the process books became too expensive for many who need them most — for the G. I.'s and their wives coming out of college, for the professional groups who are first to feel high costs. Rising costs deprive new writers of a start. They tend to place a false value on the book club adoption and the mass sale of reprints. These were worries which woke a publisher up before dawn, and Alfred McIntyre was always a light sleeper. Not once but several times I have heard him say, "I finished that manuscript between four and seven this morning." And there was a still more exacting demand on a man of his fair and liberal tendencies. He believed that the purpose of publishing was to edify quite as much as to entertain, and that it was the courage of a publisher not to follow a party line, but to reconcile, as far as books of ideas ever can, the conservatism of the Right and the extravagances of the Left — in short, to find and publish the middle course, the American course.

A program like this took courage and invited criticism, but it was Alfred's program and because of his integrity and his judgment I think we, all of us, editors and authors, and fellow publishers, continued to put more dependence upon him than one man's strength could bear.

Alfred McIntyre was so good that we should not have worn him out at sixty-two. This question of premature death in the United States we have never looked in the eye. Is it inevitable that in our more conscientious callings we should demand so much of a man in judgment, in taste, and responsibility that the piano wires of his nerves are tightened beyond release at sixty? Must we kill off under unremitting attrition our statesmen and doctors, our scientists and educators, our writers and publishers, leaders in whatever field, men who live on their nerves and who shape the decisions of a free society? Perhaps this is the cost of being right-minded, of being a leader in a time of tension. Your great fighter knows when he is taking his punishment; few American men have any illusions on that score, and certainly not Alfred McIntyre, who knew in his last summer that he was tired almost beyond recovery. But a great fighter would rather go out on his feet. **And he did.**

15
The Eyes of Texas

I made my first visit to Texas in 1935, and I've been going back at regular intervals ever since. Going back to
watch the development of what in any other continent
would be an independent nation; going back to scout for
the writers and the literature which are beginning to well
up in these resourceful plains rather less plentifully than
the oil; going back to renew my friendship with some
of the most attractive Americans I know.

The size of it, of course, is unbelievable. When I get up
high in Texas and look as far as my eye will carry across
the plains, I always expect to see the ocean at the horizon's rim. It just doesn't stand to reason that any land can
stretch as far as this without running into an ocean.

Texas has a brag all its own. Pat Neff, the former president of Baylor University, once said that Texas could wear
Rhode Island as a watch fob. There are 254 counties in
this state, and the largest, Brewster County, is actually six
times larger than Rhode Island. One county. All told,
Texas is one twelfth of the entire United States. If it had
the population density of Massachusetts, it would number
145 million people. Someday it probably will — that's

what every Texan believes — though actually, there are only something over eight million people living in this huge domain at this moment.

Eventually I came to that expanding town on the Gulf called Corpus Christi. I was met at the station by two seven-foot Texans wearing ten-gallon hats and beautifully stitched high-heeled boots. They picked up my suitcases as if they were bags of popcorn; and, feeling like a midget, I walked between the big boys up the street to the local hotel. "Are you a Moose?" they asked. "No, I'm not," I said. "Well, anyway, we're having a luncheon meeting today," they said, "and we want you to come. We'd like you to make a short speech — say about three minutes — and then we'll all listen to Judge Jones." I thanked them and said I would be delighted.

As I signed the hotel register I could hear a brass band upstairs in the ballroom playing so loudly that it made the walls palpitate. So when, after lunch, I was called on for my remarks, I said I bet I was the first Yankee that had ever been welcomed to Corpus Christi with a brass band — and sat down. They laughed at that, and then everyone settled back to hear what Judge Jones had to say.

The Judge was a big fellow with a reassuring voice. He told them that this home town of theirs, Corpus Christi, had doubled its population in two years. "We've got 50,-000 souls living here," he said, "and we're all worried about the water supply. But I can tell you men," he added, "that the plans we've just drawn up for a new reservoir will provide this town with water enough for half a million. We'll have the water in five years. Now you go out and find the people." I might add, in case you don't know it, that Corpus Christi, population now over 110,000 and going up, is a natural, one of the great boom towns, a city so rich in oil and natural gas and shipping that I have no doubt it will live up to that prophecy.

Every American loves to exaggerate. Exaggeration is an indivisible part of our humor. In Texas, where size counts so much, they make a specialty of tall stories, the kind of stories that were told about Davy Crockett who was killed in the Alamo. The most entertaining collector of these tall stories is J. Frank Dobie, who was for many years Professor of English at the University of Texas. There is, for instance, this whopper about the Bostonian who, on his first visit to Texas, found a lobster in his bed. Knowing that he was being teased, he called his host and said tactfully, "What is this — a Texas bedbug?" His host shook his head doubtfully. "Could be, but if so, it's a mighty small one."

One of my first friends in Texas was John A. Lomax of Houston, the collector of American ballads and the author of a memorable autobiography, *Adventures of a Ballad Hunter*. It was he who took me to my first Independence Day banquet (University of Texas graduates always get together on April 21); and at the dinner's end, when they stand up to sing "The Eyes of Texas Are upon You," you realize that there is a special brand of patriotism which holds together this state and empire.

Mr. Lomax's parents moved from Mississippi to Texas at the end of the Civil War. They were part of that big migration from Virginia, the Carolinas, Tennessee, and Mississippi — the hardy stock, who, in their covered wagons, became the backbone of the new state. The Lomax family built themselves a two-room house close to the old Chisholm Trail, and now I let Mr. Lomax tell the story in his own words:

I couldn't have been more than four years old when I first heard a cowboy sing and yodel to his cattle. I was sleeping in my father's two-room house — twelve of us sometimes in two rooms. Suddenly a cowboy's singing waked me as I slept on my trundle bed. A slow rain fell in the darkness outside. I listened to the patter on the pine shingles above me, and through the open window I could hear the cries of the cowboy trying to quiet, in the deep darkness and sifting rain, a trail herd of restless cattle. Over and over the fresh young voice of the cowboy rang out in the night, pleading with the cattle to lie down and sleep and not to worry:

Whoo-oo-oo-ee-oo-oo, Whoo-oo, Whoo-whoo-oo . . .
O, slow up dogies, quit your roving around.
You have wandered and tramped all over the ground;
O, graze along, dogies, and feed kinda slow,
And don't forever be on the go—
O move slow, dogies, move slow.
O, say, little dogies, when you goin' to lay down
And quit this forever a-siftin' around?
My legs are weary, my seat is sore;
O, lay down, dogies, like you've laid down before—
Lay down, little dogies, lay down.
Whoo-oo-oo-ee-oo-oo, Whoo-ee-whoo-whoo-whoo-oo.

[88]

The Eyes of Texas

"During the period of twenty years," Mr. Lomax related, "ten million cattle and a million horses were driven northward from Texas along the Chisholm Trail and other cattle trails. As the cowboys drove the cattle along, they constantly made up new songs about the trail, and these I began to write down when I was a small boy."

I used to stay with Mr. Lomax in Houston, and it was a joy to hear him tell of his early efforts to record the cowboy songs. He used to muscle in to the round-ups, and to the cowboys he was known as "The Professor with the Big Horn." Curiously enough it was his Harvard professor, George Lyman Kittredge, who put him on the trail. Mr. Lomax had worked his way through college and had then taught school to earn the money for his Ph.D. He came to Harvard, intent on doing one of those routine jobs on "Browning's Use of the Adverb" and was making heavy weather of it. One evening he paid a call on Professor Kittredge, and while he was waiting for his ring to be answered, he hummed one of his favorite songs of the range. He looked up to find Kitty standing there. "What's that you're singing?" said his professor.

"Why, sir, that's a cowboy song from Texas."

"Know any more of them?"

"Yes, sir, I've got a whole handwritten roll of them in my trunk."

"Go back and get them at once," said Kittredge with his gruff kindliness. "They may be better for you than Browning."

And that's how the research started that was to last him the rest of his life. The Library of Congress became interested; later his son Alan joined in the search, which led from the Texas plains to the Southern penitentiaries, to the waterboy, to Leadbelly, and on and on.

Texans are still so close to the past and so busy with the present that very few of them bother to write. The story of how the state was settled and then wrested away from Mexico is a fresh living memory in many families. One of my friends in Fort Worth who is not too old, likes to remember when this sprawling city of 280,000 was just a cattle town, the headquarters of the big ranch owners, with a dusty main street like any American main street leading up to the courthouse on the rise. This man's great-grandfather was the Texan ambassador to the United States when the Lone Star came into the Union. It all sounds like only yesterday, when he tells it.

The best account of how Texas began is to be found in that vivid biography of Sam Houston, *The Raven,* by Marquis James. Sam Houston was a great buffalo of a man — dark-haired, shaggy, broad-shouldered, and very handsome with his deep-set eyes. Houston was an Indian fighter and one of the heroes of the War of 1812; he was a major general and Governor of Tennessee in his early thirties. Andrew Jackson would have given him a high place in Washington. At this point in his career he married a young, somewhat delicate beauty from Mississippi. That is surely one of the most mysterious marriages in all American history. The couple separated before the honeymoon was over. Houston resigned his governorship, threw up his chance for the Senate or the Cabinet, and went back to the Indians to live with the Cherokees under an assumed name. He was never to see his wife again, and until this day we don't know what came between them.

But Houston was too big a man to hide. The Cherokees called him "the Raven"; they sent him as their representative to Washington. And so, by one of those fascinating chains of circumstances, Sam Houston, with his prodigious strength, his knowledge of Indian fighting, and his magnetism became the natural leader of Texas in its fight for independence. Sam Houston was the soldier who redeemed the Alamo, who captured the Mexican general, Santa Anna, and who served two terms as the President of Texas. His life story, as Marquis James tells it, is a book to remember.

Texas literature is ripe for the picking, but there just are not enough writers in the state to do it justice. The story of Stephen Austin, like the story of the Alamo, deserves to be written and rewritten. The story of the great plains and of the great ranches will always fire our imagination; if you haven't read one recently, look up that superb short novel *The Sea of Grass* by Conrad Richter, a story full of color and vitality.

The Texas of Roy Bedichek is not the country commonly seen by the visitors to Dallas, Houston, and Fort Worth. He prefers the unfrequented spot; and since he is a wise and perceptive naturalist, it is an adventure to follow him wherever he leads. In his book *Karánkaway Country* he explores that section of marshland lying

"slaunchwise of the compass" between Galveston and
Padre Island, once inhabited by a fierce and giant tribe
of godless Indians, and still a wildlife refuge for some of
our nearly extinct species like the whooping crane. Mr.
Bedichek has the swift observance of an Audubon and
with it an altogether fascinating knowledge of the past.
He knows the earliest chronicles of the conquering Spaniard and missionary; he knows what the lay of the land
was before oil began to contaminate the shore and the
water life; he deplores the recklessness with which we
Americans rip up our resources; he writes to defend and
to arouse, for he believes we can still strike that balance
between commercial exploitation and the preservation of
living assets which this country so badly needs.

The diversity of his interests makes his pages of constant
surprise. He writes of the droughts in Southwest Texas
where, as the local humorist puts it, bullfrogs are often
three years old before they learn to swim, and he tells
how the earlier settlers were fortified against these
droughts when a university-trained German, after study-
ing the cross-section of a one-hundred-and-thirty-year-old
post oak, proved that "moisture is the only cause of varia-
tion in tree-rings." There had been droughts here before,
many of them in the life of this tree, but they had been
followed by rain — so the settlers stayed on. He gives
fair, firm, warning of the competing interests, and of
how the gulfland oil with its poisonous "slicks" has smoth-
ered shrimp, fish, and oysters until the oyster production
has dwindled to one fifth of what it was a few years ago.
The fish and oyster industry, he reminds us, if properly

practiced, is self-renewing, though not under present con-
ditions. He speaks again and again of the Karánkaways,
who lived mainly on fish and oysters. He tells their pitiable
history as they were decimated by the bullet, the bayonet,
and whisky; of the small number of them who were
baptized *in articulo mortis;* and of how the last remnant of
the tribe was finally moved to Mexico a hundred years
ago. There were then eight individuals left; now they are
gone for good, and only bitter memories of them remain.

Mr. Bedichek has eyes for natural phenomena great and
small, for the wolves and the coyotes, the wild hogs and
the snakes, but the birds are his heart's delight. His account of the meadow larks on a spring morning is Texas
poetry of the best — so is his affectionate observation of
the scissortails. With Tom Waddell, the game warden,
he watches the courting of the prairie chickens, and then
Tom begins to speak of the "grand free-for-all competition" in killing the prairie chickens which was part of the
frontier Fourth of July and which still persists in modified
form. When Mr. Bedichek writes that the whooping crane
has a voice which carries three miles and a wingspread
measuring seven and a half feet, he tells me something
new, but when he tells me that there are only thirty-six
of them left and that, like the Karánkaways, they will
soon be extinct, the story takes on poignancy. In short,
this is an observant, telling book, salty with experiences
but made deeply sympathetic by a man who rebels against
the ruthless destruction of American aborigines, man or
beast.

16

The Gentlest Art

E. V. Lucas called letter writing "the gentlest art" and he used that phrase as a title for one of the most delightful of anthologies, *The Gentlest Art: A Choice of Letters by Entertaining Hands*. This anthology was three times reprinted, a success which led to a second volume called *The Second Post*. Both were published before the First World War; both reflect the serenity of Victoria's and Edward's England; both reflect the affectionate, high-spirited, often passionate individualism of men and women reaching across the silence of space for the sympathy of that other heart. And both can still be purchased in any good secondhand bookshop.

These were the letter writers who most appealed to Mr. Lucas: he liked the self-contemplation of Robert Louis Stevenson (to me Stevenson's letters sound as if they were written before a mirror); he liked the warm geniality of Charles Lamb, the cool-eyed observation of Shelley (who was more impassioned in his poetry than in his prose); he liked the tart, impudent, confiding revelations of Lord Byron, and the eager devotion of John

Keats as he writes down his love for the two women who
matter most to him — Fanny Keats, his younger sister, and
Fanny Brawne.

You feel these letters *had* to be written. They are the
instant expression of a mood that could not wait: "Pray
do write to me," says Edward FitzGerald; "a few lines
soon are better than a three-decker a month hence." Some
of these letters run long; some are only two lines; some
are working on the surface; some, like Dean Swift's to
Stella, are so charged with intimacy and association that
no living detective has found their full message.

Here, for instance, is Dick Steele, junior partner of that
famous editorial team Addison and Steele, writing in
chains. He is writing to "Dear, lovely Mrs. Scurlock," and
he says:

SMITH STREET, WESTMINSTER, 1707

MADAM, — I lay down last night with your image in my
thoughts, and have awak'd this morning in the same contemplation. The pleasing transport with which I'me delighted, has a sweetnesse in it attended with a train of ten
thousand soft desires, anxieties, and cares; the day arises on
my hopes with new brightnesse; youth, beauty and innocence are the charming objects that steal me from myself,
and give me joys above the reach of ambition, pride or
glory. Beleive me, fair one, to throw myself at your feet
is giving my self the highest blisse I know on Earth. Oh
hasten ye minutes! bring on the happy morning wherein to
be ever her's will make me look down on thrones! Dearest
Prue, I am tenderly, passionately, faithfully thine,

RICHARD STEELE

Books *and* Men

SATURDAY NIGHT (*Aug.* 30, 1707)

DEAR, LOVELY MRS. SCURLOCK, — I have been in very good company, where your health, under the character of the woman I lov'd best, has been often drunk, so that I may say I am dead drunk for your sake, which is more than I die for you.

—Yours, R. STEELE

ST. JAMES'S COFFEE-HOUSE
Sept. 1, 1707

MADAM, — It is the hardest thing in the world to be in love and yet to attend to businesse. As for me, all who speake to me find me out, and I must lock myself up, or other people will do it for me. A gentleman ask'd me this morning what news from Lisbon, and I answer'd she's exquisitely handsome. Another desir'd to know when I had been last at Hampton Court, I reply'd 'Twill be on Tuesday come se'nnight.' Prithee allow me at least to kisse your hand before that day, that my mind may be in some composure. O love!

A thousand torments dwell about thee,
Yet who would live to live without thee?

Methinks I could write a volume to you, but all the language on earth would fail in saying how much, and with what disinterested passion, I am ever yours,

RICHD. STEELE

[Steele and his Prue were married on September 9, 1707.]

March 11, 1708-9

DEAR PRUE, — I enclose five guineas, but can't come home

to dinner. Dear little woman, take care of thyself, and eat and drink cheerfully.

RICHD. STEELE

Sept. 30, 1710

DEAR PRUE, — I am very sleepy and tired, but could not think of closing my eyes till I had told you I am, dearest creature, your most affectionate and faithful husband,

RICHARD STEELE

From the Press one in the morning.

March 28, 1713

DEAR PRUE, — I will do every thing you desire your own way.

— Yours ever, RICHARD STEELE

Compare this domesticity with Shelley's account of his visit to Lord Byron in Ravenna in 1821:

Lord Byron is in excellent cue both of health and spirits. He has got rid of all those melancholy and degrading habits which he indulged at Venice. He lives with one woman, a lady of rank here (Countess Guiccioli), to whom he is attached, and who is attached to him, and is in every respect an altered man. He has written three more cantos of 'Don Juan.' I have yet only heard the fifth, and I think that every word of it is pregnant with immortality. . . . Lord Byron gets up at *two* (P.M.). I get up, quite contrary to my usual custom, but one must sleep or die, like Southey's sea-snake in 'Kehama,' at 12. After breakfast we sit talking till six. From six till eight we gallop through the pine forests which divide Ravenna from the sea; we then come home and dine, and sit up gossiping till six in the morning. I don't suppose this will kill me in a week or fortnight, but I shall not try it longer. Lord B.'s establishment consists, besides servants, of ten horses, eight enormous dogs, three monkeys, five cats, an eagle, a crow, and a falcon; and all these, except the horses, walk about the house, which every now and then resounds with their unarbitrated quarrels, as if they were the masters of it.

Byron's letters of the very same period to Murray and Hobhouse are sardonic, sulphuric, completely candid in his growing impatience with the Countess, whom he cannot bring himself to leave, premonitory as when he declares how old he feels, and pathetic in his unphrased desire to regain England's respect. If Byron is rated the greatest letter writer in English literature — and there are many who so consider him — it is because he wrote himself down so naturally, so unsparingly, and with that extraordinary mixture of feelings which was his character. He never wrote self-consciously, as if posterity were looking over his shoulder.

This incidentally cannot be said of one of the remarkable letter writers of our time, T. E. Lawrence. Lawrence maintained a wide-ranging correspondence, and his letters — whether from the desert, Peace Conference or tank corps — were probably the most brilliant to emerge from the First World War. But it is a curious thing that Lawrence had no compunction about writing the identical episode almost word for word to a number of friends. And the repetition, as if one could not make too much of a good thing, became something of a public literary exercise.

Personally I should place Keats's letters on the same

shelf with Byron's. They each brought to their correspondence the openness, the intimacy, and the essence of the
individual, which show the man plain. There is a wide
range in Keats's writing: the refreshing gaiety as he tells
of his walking trip in Scotland with Brown; the sorrow as
when he writes of Tom's death; the teasing, half-serious
manner as he writes to George and Georgiana Keats in
America describing his first meeting with Miss Brawne;
his candor, as when he tells the reproachful artist Haydon,
to whom he has loaned £30, that he is penniless and
can lend him no more; the eager letters looking ahead to
the writing which he hoped to complete, and the last
letters to Fanny Brawne, which even at this distance go
through the reader "like a spear."

It was Christopher Morley, lecturing in the Harvard
Union in 1920 when I was an undergraduate, who first
led me to read Keats's poems against the eager, passionate
commitment of his letters. I can think of no more awaken-
ing experience for one who is fresh and ready for poetry.

17

The Building of the *Times*

THE New York *Times,* which celebrated its centennial in 1951, was built up to be the best newspaper in America in the short span of sixteen years. It was a decrepit and failing property when, in 1896, Adolph S. Ochs bought it for $75,000. In the first year, Mr. Ochs made the innovations and defined the policy which has ever since been its guiding light; in a matter of months he had brought it back into active competition with its leading competitors, the *Tribune,* the *Herald,* and the *World,* and from that time until the sinking of the *Titanic* in 1912, the *Times* was in the ascendant. Its coverage of the *Titanic* disaster made publishing history and shot it into a lead it has never relinquished. The two men chiefly responsible for this were Mr. Ochs and his incomparable Managing Editor, Carr Van Anda. How they worked together, how they set their standards and built up their staff, how they made the *Times* the most dependable newspaper of record in the world, has been well told by Meyer Berger in *The Story of the New York Times, 1851-1951.*

In the light of its success it is amusing to recall what a hard time the *Times* had getting on its feet. Beginning in 1813 seven different proprietors struggled to establish in

The Building of the Times

Manhattan a paper with this name at the masthead, and seven times they failed. The eighth to try was Henry Jarvis Raymond, a wiry, energetic, politically active editor who got his *Times* off to a solid start in 1851, a conservative penny paper in a two-cent market then dominated by Horace Greeley's *Tribune,* James Gordon Bennett's *Herald,* and James Watson Webb's *Courier and Enquirer.*

Long-lived periodicals have their ups and downs, and the *Times's* circulation had shrunk to 9000 copies when in August, 1896, Adolph S. Ochs became its owner. There were then fifteen newspapers in the city, with Pulitzer's *World,* in its morning and evening editions, leading the field with a total circulation of 600,000. The *Times* was in last place, and no one could then have suspected that Ochs would live to see the day when all but the *Times* had died or been absorbed in mergers.

Adolph S. Ochs was the son of a German immigrant, and his success story is better than anything out of Horatio Alger, because, as I remember, Alger's heroes did not perform their miracles with huge debts on both shoulders. "Mooley" Ochs, as he was called, quit school at fourteen to become a chore boy for the Knoxville *Chronicle.* He lived on a shoestring; he was tireless, he impressed people with his direct honesty, and he never backed down on a promise. By twenty he had risen from printer's devil to be the publisher and editor of the wobbly Chattanooga *Times,* then selling barely 250 copies a day. He needed loans, and big ones, to install new machinery and to build up the paper. But loans, however sizable, never fazed him nor watered his judgment, either in the South or in the crucial days in New York when, after the building of the new Times Tower in 1905, he had to put up 51 per cent of the *Times* stock for a loan of $300,000.

When he took control of the New York *Times,* he made certain small changes which were characteristic and lasting. He threw out the cheap backstair fiction; he made the format more readable, widening the space between the lines of type and using better newsprint and ink to obtain a sharper reproduction. He chose the slogan "All the News That's Fit to Print," and he added an illustrated half-tone Sunday supplement and a book review section. He had an inexhaustible curiosity about the unmapped areas of the world and the unknown in science. Over the years he built up the largest, most capable news-gathering staff in the country, and at its head was Carr Van Anda.

There never has been a Managing Editor to touch Van Anda, and the twenty-one years in which he set the tone and the pace of the *Times* is an epic story in itself. It was Van Anda who deduced from the first fragmentary wireless message the fact that the *Titanic* was not only in trouble but that she had sunk. Where other editors played it safe, awaiting confirmation from the White Star Line, he acted on cold reasoning. He immediately planned a round-up of the survivors' stories with sixteen reporters operating from a field office close to the *Carpathia's* dock. Years later, when Van Anda was visiting Lord Northcliffe, the London editor pulled open a desk drawer. In it lay the New York *Times* for April 19, 1912. "We keep this,"

he said, "as an example of the greatest accomplishment
of news reporting."

It was Van Anda who in 1908 secured a blistering,
belligerent interview with the Kaiser, and then had the
sense of honor and good faith not to let it be published —
for in those pre-Vishinsky days such flaming words might
well have brought on war. It was Van Anda who refused
to follow Roy Howard's premature Armistice story of
November 7, 1918; Van Anda who monopolized the only
two phones out of Plymouth, Vermont, the night Cal
Coolidge took the oath.

The policies and traditions of the *Times* attracted the
best: Garet Garrett, Wythe Williams, and Charles Grasty
in the First World War; Hanson Baldwin, the ace military
commentator, backed by an incomparable team of corre-
spondents, in the Second. Alexander Woollcott and Brooks
Atkinson on the theater, Waldemar Kaempffert and William L. Laurence in science, Arthur Krock and James B.
Reston in Washington, John H. Finley, Lester Markel,
and Charles Merz as editors, Simeon Strunsky and Anne
O'Hare McCormick on the editorial page — these are a
few of the many who poured their talents into the im-
personal eminence of the *Times.* Other papers — the
Tribune, for instance — have encouraged a more individual style. Hearst in his short hard-bitten paragraphing set
a pattern that could be more easily read and more highly
colored. The *Times,* on through the present regime of
Arthur H. Sulzberger, President and Publisher, has maintained its sovereignty by a comprehension of detail, an

unflurried judgment, and a style as quiet as it is authoritative. There can be wastage in such writing, and the *Times's* stories sometimes run to excessive length. There is also a tendency to be aloof, so that the picaresque or bizarre doings of Babylon on the Hudson are recounted in much the same manner as a report of opinions handed down by the Supreme Court. But these are minor matters in an era of highly tempered and angled news.

Meyer Berger, a member of the staff, has told the story as a great reporter should tell it — graphically, self-effacingly, and with a warmhearted enthusiasm for the great undertaking which soon kindles the reader's sympathy. His book is a masterly achievement in thoroughness, authority, and readability. It makes me live again in the high points of the first half-century; it makes me appreciate the spell, the excitement, and the hardheaded pursuit of truth which is journalism at its best.

The Literary Supplement of the New York *Times* has been the Bible of the book trade for as long as I can remember. To celebrate their part in the Centennial, the literary editors have gone back to their files to reprint with contemporary illustrations the *Times* reviews of the most famous books of the past century, more than one hundred volumes, as they were judged in their first flush of publication. What strikes me at once is the justness, the permanent common sense of the *Times's* attitude toward these books that made history. To us, of course, these novelists like Joyce and Proust, these men of ideas like Darwin and Marx, these poets like Whitman, Kipling,

Amy Lowell, are known quantities — labeled and in place. We read with hindsight what these critics were writing with foresight, and the result is to me a competitive and fascinating commentary on modern literature.

Here, for instance, is Joseph Collins, with his two superb reviews of *Ulysses* and *Swann's Way,* both published in 1922; both admirable interpretations of a way of writing utterly strange to most of us then, however familiar it may have become since. Collins had what seems to me the essential qualities for a first-class reviewer: a fresh, open, associative mind; taste, sympathy, and a good sense of proportion. *Ulysses* he rates as "the most important contribution that has been made to fictional literature in the Twentieth Century." It took courage to say so then and he was right.

The appraisals of Darwin's *Origin of Species,* of E. M. Forster's *Passage to India,* and of *Mein Kampf* seem to me equally laudable. Naturally you would expect good things when Brander Matthews in 1919 gives you his opinion of Henry Mencken's *The American Language,* or when Mencken gives you his of Dreiser's novel, *The Financier.* But most of these come from anonymous pens.

The most spectacular misses occur in the fields of political economy, morality, and poetry. *The Economic Consequences of the Peace* by John Maynard Keynes is dismissed as an "acrimonious party pamphlet," and *Das Kapital* as "resulting from an excess of spleen." Dickens is praised for his "acceptance in a cheerful spirit of things as they are"; Zola is solemnly told that his novel, *Les Rougon-Macquart,* "may become an agency of immorality without being immoral itself"; Thomas Mann, that he isn't in a class with Galsworthy; and Taine, that he is "specious and fanciful." Carl Sandburg and Amy Lowell ("her whole book is of the veritable stuff of dreams") are praised to the skies, while Baudelaire, Yeats, and T. S. Eliot are scanted. The philosophers fare the best: Bergson, William James, Spengler, Nietzsche, and John Dewey are well described and accurately weighed.

On the evidence, these reviewers are writing for a public that has grown in sophistication. There is an increasing use of descriptive shorthand, an increasing avoidance of cliches, a gain in terseness and more directness. These of course are picked reviews of major books; and as you mull them over, you are reminded of the flaws in contemporary reviewing: the tendency to turn the review into a news story, or if it be of a novel, the temptation to skeletonize the plot; the tendency of young reviewers to be cleverly disparaging of older, long-established writers — Mazo de la Roche, Kenneth Roberts, the late James Hilton were three typical victims — and, most blameworthy of all, a kind of guarded deference toward those big blowsy novels (with plenty of advertising behind them) that really ought to be scorched. The best critics on the *Times* are never deferential.

The steadily rising cost of operating a metropolitan daily, the tendency of advertisers to support only the leader, and the encroaching competition with radio and television have had a deadly effect on journalism: of the American newspapers which were in print in 1929, 40 per cent have either perished or been absorbed by their larger rival. The consolidation which emerges, usually with a radio station in tow, is inclined to play it safe, to reach for a lower common denominator of interest. In this process, which of course continues, we have lost the independence and quality which were once to be found in the New York *World* and the New York *Evening Sun,* the Boston *Evening Transcript* and the Brooklyn *Daily Eagle,* to name but four. But this crushing effect of the mass medium has not deterred the proprietors of the New York *Times.* While the *Times* could borrow to its advantage from the crusading liberalism of the St. Louis *Post Dispatch,* from the sensitive, intelligent probing of racial issues of the Louisville *Courier-Journal,* and from the brilliant, individual writing of the New York *Herald Tribune,* in its own uncompromising standards and integrity the New York *Times* unquestionably sets the pace.

18

A New York Editor:
Maxwell E. Perkins

THERE is an old saying, "Scratch an editor and you'll find a disappointed writer." Nothing could be further from the truth. In the very nature of his work, a good editor can not be a disappointed man; he must be a hopeful man. He must have an insatiable zest for reading, and he must wake up every morning, week ends included, with the hope that in the reading of this day he will discover new talent.

A good editor is half critic, half writer; he should have the ability to detect the strength as well as the weakness in any manuscript, and to help amplify that strength when need be. Finally, and most important of all, a good editor is instinctive: he has the instinctive ability to put himself in the author's place, and the creative power — not as much as the author's, of course, but enough — to help project that vision of the book the author has seen in his mind.

This instinct was highly developed in Maxwell E. Perkins, who was for thirty-seven years an editor of Charles Scribner's Sons, for the last fifteen of these its editor in chief. Max Perkins was, as his associate, John Hall

A New York Editor: Maxwell E. Perkins

Wheelock, fairly says, "the most creative editor of his time," and to read his perceptive, warmhearted correspondence, *Editor to Author,* is to realize why a good editor in the heat of his occupation seldom has time to write anything but letters. He has given the full strength of his imagination to the kindling of other people's books.

Like all great editors, Max never had enough of his work. He got to the office at nine in the morning or earlier, worked a long day, and avoided like death the literary cocktail parties whose leaden after-effects would have ruined his evening's reading. No week end was ever long enough for the manuscripts he took home in his briefcase. He begrudged himself a ten-day vacation, and couldn't understand why his secretary or anyone else in the office wanted more. Once, after a particularly hard spot of work, he allowed himself to be tempted down to Key West by Ernest Hemingway. The first day, Hemingway took him out on the water and Max caught a fish. That evening they sat together drinking and talking over books and the manuscripts to come, but it was only a matter of days before Max was homesick for his work, and back he came two weeks before any associate expected him.

I remember Max in his office. It was a plain little room high up on the corner of 48th Street with the current of Fifth Avenue surging below. Max, a slender, neat figure, with taffy coloring, a Greek profile and a quiet voice, worked with a bare desk, perhaps a pad and a few penciled notes — no more. He worked with his hat on, a brown felt hat which must have changed through the years but which always looked the same. Every editor has to cope with a certain number of wound-up visitors, and rumor had it that Max wore his hat to give these long talkers the impression he was about to leave for an appointment. But time was something he never begrudged to those he believed in.

Since few readers ever identify the publishers of their favorite books, let me enumerate some of the talented writers whom Max attracted and helped to develop under the Scribner imprint. He discovered F. Scott Fitzgerald; he found Ring Lardner in journalism, and brought Lardner's stories together in book form; he recognized the enormous potential of Thomas Wolfe, after Tom's first novel had been declined by several publishers, and to the editing of *Look Homeward, Angel* and *Of Time and the River,* he devoted the hardest hours of his career; he coaxed and braced Marjorie Kinnan Rawlings to write *The Yearling,* when others were after her for a more commercial novel. With his love of American history he brought knowledgeable help to the historical novels of James Boyd; to the picturesque books of John W. Thomason, Jr., the gifted Marine; to Will James, the cowboy, and to the historical sequence by Marcia Davenport. He edited Erskine Caldwell, the mysteries of S. S. Van Dine, and every big novel of Ernest Hemingway. No other American editor could match this list for its talent and its diversity.

The letters which have been gathered together in *Editor to Author* show the diversity; they show Max Perkins's magnetic capacity for appreciation, the devotion to detail, the wise and listening sympathy, and the shy Yankee diffidence with which Max made his constructive suggestions. The letters have that absorbing, intimate, revealing quality which is the hallmark of every great letter writer. Whether he is counseling a young novelist or advising an elder on his autobiography, or breaking the truth of slow sales to as touchy a subject as John Galsworthy, his words are direct, masculine, and considerate. And above all — this is the point I hope readers (and younger editors) will bear in mind — he was never didactic; he gave his criticism and his suggestions in such a tentative way that the author never felt that he was being censored or his authority challenged.

"Do not ever defer to my judgment," he wrote to Scott Fitzgerald. "You won't on any vital point, I know, and I should be ashamed, if it were possible to have made you . . ." Yet later, when they were going over the manuscript of Fitzgerald's best book, *The Great Gatsby,* it was Max who put his finger on the unnatural mysteriousness which surrounded Gatsby, and with his criticism helped to clear the fog away.

To Edward Bok, who was finishing the last volume of his autobiography, he wrote: "I think your books as a whole run the danger of giving the impression that you overvalue *material* success. This book does not, perhaps, as it stands; but, at the same time . . ." and again, he was probing for ways to correct that impression. To James Boyd, who had just finished the manuscript of that fine Revolutionary novel, *Drums,* Max wrote: "In all my comments, my idea is not so much that there are deficiencies, but that you have abilities that might get fuller play."

And to Marjorie Kinnan Rawlings he gave this advice: "The sales department always want a novel. They want to turn everything into a novel. They would have turned the New Testament into one, if it had come to us for publication, and they could have. But I am right about it, and a book about a boy and the life of the scrub is the thing we want. Anyhow, the thing for you to do is to write it as you feel it and want it, without regard to anybody at all. It is those wonderful river trips, and the hunting, and the dogs and guns, and the companionship of simple people who care about the same things which were included in *South Moon Under* that we are thinking about. It is all simple, not complicated — don't let anything make it complicated to you."

The vigilance with which Max detected the soft spots in any manuscript, and the imagination with which he helped to sustain the best work of his authors, naturally attracted to him many, many aspirants. His letters of rejection are a remarkable blend of firmness and humility, particularly that letter written toward the close of his life to the enraged writer who felt that Scribner's was depriving her of her right to give the world a message — the letter in which he says: "You ask who I am, and I may as well answer you and have an end to it. I am, or at least should be if I fulfilled myself, John Smith, U.S.A. He is the man who doesn't know much, nor think that he knows much. He starts out with certain ambitions but he gradually accumulates obligations as he goes along . . ." That, I think, is one of the greatest letters Max ever wrote.

A New York Editor: Maxwell E. Perkins

The friendship which grows out of the author-editor relationship sometimes develops a dependency. There are dangers in this, as Max well knew, and in his diffident way he tried to avoid them, but they could not be avoided in the case of Tom Wolfe. Wolfe's first novel, *Look Homeward, Angel,* called for an immense amount of editing. I doubt if the book would have been so successful without the work Perkins put into it. A more difficult problem presented itself in Wolfe's still larger novel, *Of Time and the River.* When the manuscript was in its next to final stage, the author felt impelled to inject throughout a Marxian philosophy which had not been in his thoughts when he first conceived and wrote the story, and which in Perkins's judgment was foreign to the character of the book. Perkins, who had many books on the fire in this particular year, was giving Wolfe two hours every night while this controversy raged, and for long periods they would sit in silence glowering at the manuscript and occasionally at each other. Finally Wolfe said, "Well, then you will take the responsibility?" Perkins replied, "I have simply got to take the responsibility. And what's more," he added, "I will be blamed either way." And he was. For although Wolfe dedicated this novel to his editor in words which still glow, it was the last of his to appear under the Scribner imprint. He took his next novel to Harper's, where, I may add, it received just as toilsome a going-over.

There are many other literary controversies which are met with courage in these letters. We see how Max stood up to the onslaught of the Christian Scientists at the time Scribner's published its new biography of Mary Baker

Eddy. We see his remarkable letters on the freedom of expression, as when he defends the "realism" of novelists such as Hemingway and Fitzgerald. We see his concern for libel and authors' debts. We see him deal with writers as far apart as Trotsky and Arthur Train. We are grateful to his fellow editor, John Hall Wheelock, who selected and mounted these letters about which I have only one small regret. I think Max would have permitted us to see a few of his mistakes. For no editor is infallible.

19
The Essay

THE essay is as unpredictable as it is endearing. It is a
thing of moods, gay, laughing, or satirical; it can be as
highly serious as T. S. Eliot, as didactic as Machiavelli, as
cool as Francis Bacon. It can be a confession of self; or a
swift elucidation in biography; or Virginia Woolf con-
templating a moth. In happy, relaxed times it is man
employing his senses to the nth degree, as when W. H.
Hudson, with eyes closed, walked about London guided
by his sense of smell. It is as critical as Edmund Wilson
and as full of will and wish as William James. It is
Emerson, Thoreau, William Hazlitt, Charles Lamb, or
E. B. White. It is of such calm, touching beauty that the
eyes can hardly read it aloud without weeping; it is as
derisive as Henry Mencken and as beautifully lucid as
Anne Morrow Lindbergh; it is one heart speaking to another.

Can it be all these things and still be a disciplined form
of writing? It can. It is much more imaginative than its
hard-working cousin, the magazine article; it does not deal
in statistics or belabor an argument as does a magazine
article. It does not depend on a cast of characters and a
contrived ending as does a short story. The essay is an
experience which you the reader share with the writer —

you share his laughter, delight, or pity; you share a deepened understanding or a quickening of the spirit in a style that does not date. If an essay has found truth, that truth lives on as it does in a poem; and what Hazlitt has to say about an actor was as true of Edmund Booth as it is of Charles Laughton or Alec Guinness.

The essay may be the result of long brooding, but in the writing it is short. This limitation imposes upon the essayist the necessity of winning the confidence of the reader in a very few sentences: the first two pages set the subject and evoke the mood. The opening is decisive.

Dr. Johnson defined the essay as "a loose sally of the mind," and the early exponents of the art, from Montaigne to Robert Louis Stevenson, addressed themselves to the reader in a personal and familiar way. Thus the familiar essay was established as the classic essay, charming or pensive, confessional or in protest or exhortation. The joy of the medium is that it offers such a limitless variety to the writer. Charles Lamb can write wistfully of *Dream Children,* the children whom, because of the insanity of his sister, he never had; Macaulay can flash on you his strongly, brilliantly opinionated judgment of Lord Clive; Evelyn can tell you of his Garden, and Henry Thoreau explain why he has renounced Concord and the larger universe for a hut beside Walden Pond. The one constant in all this is that each page is indelibly marked with personality. Style is at once the man himself and the shimmering costume of words which centers your attention. I can think of ranking novelists — Theodore Dreiser is one — whose style was as commonplace as a newspaper article; but I cannot name a single essayist who has survived without this evocative magic. Style is the very breath of the essay; it is an invitation and an enchantment; it is that skillful and disarming use of words which makes friends out of strangers — which makes you the reader say to yourself, "Now there's a writer I'd really like to know. It would be fun to live with him." And then you do live with him, for a time, vicariously.

Since 1914 a note of anxiety has been struck with increasing frequency — anxiety about the present and apprehension of the future. As writers became more worried, they abandoned the light play of ideas; they became more objective, more formal, and they took themselves more seriously. Bertrand Russell was awarded the Nobel Prize in large measure because of his piercing, provocative essays; and if you will read his volume entitled *Unpopular Essays,* you will hear with great preciseness this note of anxiety and warning.

As disturbance followed disturbance — war, dictatorship, the uprooting of peoples, the collapse of empires — Americans especially realized they were uninformed about a vast new range of subjects. They turned to magazines and to books for the information and the guidance which they needed. In these recurring crises, the informative article — with its statistics, dogmatic opinion, and tightly drawn conclusions — crowded out the essay. The essayist of today is facing a much more ruthless competition than those of the nineteenth century — and he knows it. He is writing for the very life of his medium. And in this state what he writes is more intense, more hilarious, more serious, or more fanciful than what he might have written in a kinder time.

This I think will be apparent as we sample the remarkable versatility of our contemporary writers. Suppose we begin with the biographical essay. I think of those glittering pieces in *Eminent Victorians* by Lytton Strachey. I think of that more imaginative collection of essays, *Seven Men* by Max Beerbohm. And of Beerbohm's penetrating portrait of the captive poet Swinburne, in the essay which he entitled: "No. 2, The Pines."

It might be well to draw a comparison here. In 1824, William Hazlitt published his famous paper "On Actors and Acting"; and from it, I take these memorable lines:

Actors have been accused, as a profession, of being extravagant and dissipated . . . it is not to be wondered at. They live from hand to mouth: they plunge from want into luxury; they have no means of making money *breed,* and all professions that do not live by turning money into money, or have not a certainty of accumulating it in the end by parsimony, spend it. Uncertain of the future, they make sure of the present moment. . . . An actor, to be a good one, must have a great spirit of enjoyment in himself, strong impulses, strong passions, and a strong sense of pleasure: for it is his business to imitate the passions, and to communicate pleaure to others. A man of genius is not a machine. The neglected actor may be excused if he drinks oblivion of his disappointments; the successful one, if he quaffs the applause of the world.

The Essay

Those words of William Hazlitt's are written with the objectivity and contemplation of the nineteenth century.

Now turn to one of our most subjective writers, Virginia Woolf, who gives us her impression of William Hazlitt himself:

Hazlitt's essays are emphatically himself. He has no reticence and he has no shame. He tells us exactly what he thinks, and he tells us — the confidence is less seductive — exactly what he feels. As of all men he had the most intense consciousness of his own existence, since never a day passed without inflicting on him some pang of hate or of jealousy, some thrill of anger or of pleasure, we cannot read him for long without coming in contact with a very singular character — ill-conditioned yet high-minded; mean yet noble; intensely egotistical, yet inspired by the most genuine passion for the rights and liberties of mankind.

Soon, so thin is the veil of the essay as Hazlitt wore it, his very look comes before us. We see him as Coleridge saw him, "brow-hanging, shoe-contemplative, strange." He comes shuffling into the room, he looks nobody straight in the face, he shakes hands with the fin of a fish; occasionally he darts a malignant glance from his corner. Yet now and again his face lit up with intellectual beauty, and his manner became radiant with sympathy and understanding. Soon, too, as we read on, we become familar with the whole gamut of his grudges and his grievances. He lived, one gathers, mostly at inns. No woman's form graced his board. He had quarrelled with all his old friends, save perhaps with Lamb. He was the object of malignant persecution — *Blackwood's* reviewers called him 'pimply Hazlitt' though his cheek was pale as alabaster. He had — no one would deny it — one of the finest minds, and he wrote indisputably the best prose style of his time. But what did that avail with women? Fine ladies have no respect for scholars, nor chambermaids either — so the growl and plaint of his grievances keeps breaking through, disturbing us, irritating us; and yet there is something so independent, subtle, fine, and enthusiastic about him — when he can forget himself he is so rapt in ardent speculation about other things — that dislike crumbles and turns to something much warmer and more complex."

Virginia Woolf, of course, never saw this man she was writing about, but you feel at once the subtle perception with which she reanimates him from the past.

Closely akin to the biographical essay is that which deals with the creative process. There is no better book on writing in the English language than that which Somerset Maugham wrote about his youth and apprenticeship. He calls it *The Summing Up* — and what else is it but a wise, sensitive and extended essay? We have an American woman to thank for another fine work in this field. I have never known her name, but it seems that on a sudden impulse she wrote to the English poet A. E. Housman asking him to define poetry and please tell her how it was he wrote his own poems. Mr. Housman, who was a crusty, withdrawn scholar, took a little time to recover from this assault on his privacy, but eventually he did write out his answer in the form of an essay on *The Name and Nature of Poetry;* and it is certainly one of the most illuminating accounts we have ever had of a poet in

action. I shall quote two passages from it. First, this question of what is poetry.

A year or two ago I received from America a request that
I would define poetry. I replied that I could no more define
poetry than a terrier can define a rat, but that I thought we
both recognized the object by the symptoms which it provokes
in us. One of these symptoms was described in connexion with
another object by Eliphaz the Temanite: "A spirit passed
before my face: the hair of my flesh stood up." Experience
has taught me, when I am shaving of a morning, to keep
watch over my thoughts, because, if a line of poetry strays
into my memory, my skin bristles so that the razor ceases to
act. This particular symptom is accompanied by a shiver down
the spine; there is another which consists in a constriction of
the throat and a precipitation of water to the eyes; and there
is a third which I can only describe by borrowing a phrase
from one of Keats' last letters, where he says, speaking of
Fanny Brawne, "everything that reminds me of her goes
through me like a spear." The seat of this sensation is the pit
of the stomach.

A little later in his essay, Mr. Housman has this to say
about his own verse: "I have seldom written poetry unless
I was rather out of health, and the experience, though
pleasurable, was generally agitating and exhausting. If
only that you may know what to avoid, I will give some
account of the process."

Having drunk a pint of beer at luncheon — beer is a seda-
tive to the brain, and my afternoons are the least intellectual
portion of my life — I would go out for a walk of two or

three hours. As I went along, thinking of nothing in particular, only looking at things around me and following the progress of the seasons, there would flow into my mind, with sudden and unaccountable emotion, sometimes a line or two of verse, sometimes a whole stanza at once, accompanied, not preceded, by a vague notion of the poem which they were destined to form part of. Then there would usually be a lull of an hour or so, then perhaps the spring would bubble up again. I say bubble up, because so far as I could make out, the source of the suggestions thus proffered to the brain was an abyss which I have already had occasion to mention, the pit of the stomach. When I got home I wrote them down, leaving gaps, and hoping that further inspiration might be forthcoming another day. Sometimes it was, if I took my walks in a receptive and expectant frame of mind; but sometimes the poem had to be taken in hand and completed by the brain, which was apt to be a matter of trouble and anxiety, involving trial and disappointment, and sometimes ending in failure. I happen to remember distinctly the genesis of the piece which stands last in *A Shropshire Lad.* Two of the stanzas, I do not say which, came into my head, just as they are printed, while I was crossing the corner of Hampstead Heath between the Spaniard's Inn and the footpath to Temple Fortune. A third stanza came with a little coaxing after tea. One more was needed, but it did not come: I had to turn to and compose it myself, and that was a laborious business. I wrote it thirteen times, and it was more than a twelvemonth before I got it right.

The biographical essay has been greatly enriched, in our time especially by the English. We Americans, it seems to me, have excelled in humor — humor which can be gentle, ironic, wonderfully exaggerated, beautifully deadpan.

I remember a week end in mid-April I spent in North Wales. It was lambing time, and the slopes of the great Welsh pastures were alive with lambs, black lambs, white lambs with black faces, the friskiest I have ever seen. I remember in one pasture watching two lambs in hot pursuit of a rabbit, and the rabbit wasn't fooling. He was getting out of there as fast as he could. The scene put me in mind of E. B. White's description of spring in that delightful book of his, *One Man's Meat*.

The intoxication of spring is a figure of speech to most creatures, but to a lamb it means a real drunk. The very young lambs who stick to a straight milk diet keep their feet pretty well, but the older ones (the ones of high school age) stagger back from the pasture and after weaving about the barnyard for a few minutes collapse. They froth at the mouth, and you can hear them grind their teeth forty feet away. It is a glorious jag, this spring drunk. I keep my syringe loaded with tea, and administer it — between paragraphs — to the worst cases. This year is not as bad as last year, for I have fewer lambs and more tea.

And having written that vernal paragraph, Mr. White goes on to add, "Whenever I tell about spring, or any delights which I experience, or the pleasant country, I think of a conversation I had with a friend in the city shortly before I left. 'I trust,' he said with an ugly leer, 'that you will spare the reading public your little adventures in contentment.'"

He is a remarkably versatile essayist, this man E. B.

White. In conferring an honorary degree upon him, President Pusey of Harvard referred to him as "the Sidewalk Superintendent of our Times," meaning the city loiterer who stands beside the evacuation for a new building and watches life through the knothole and reports.

Mr. White is a pensive observer, he is a brooder, a satirist, and in his quiet way as sympathetic an essayist as we have ever produced. In his short papers he has set the tone of the *New Yorker* since its first year of publication; his editorials on its opening page have been published anonymously but anyone who knows his style could pick them out. I remember a piece he wrote about *Who's Who in America. Who's Who* had evidently sent him a blank to fill out with his own activities, and this led him to draw the following self-portrait: "A biographee of no small inactivity ourself, we can state positively that we are under no pressure at the moment — except the tiny pressure connected with writing this ephemeral paragraph. After it is done, we intend to walk slowly to Central Park in the mild sunshine and visit the baby camel for a routine checkup, then to a saloon, where we shall pass the early afternoon hours in deep torpor over a glass of May wine — a biographee as near inert as a horned toad."

There is your sidewalk superintendent. But don't think for a minute that Mr. White is always as casual as he appears in those words. He is a moralist whose hatred of brutality and abhorrence of war speaks for us all. In his book, *The Second Tree from the Corner,* is this fine paragraph of identification: "Our own earth-bound life is schizophrenic. Half the time we feel blissfully wedded to the modern scene, in love with its every mood, amused by its every joke, imperturbable in the face of its threat, bent on enjoying it to the hilt. The other half of the time we are the fusspot moralist, suspicious of all progress, resentful of change, determined to right wrongs, correct injustices, and save the world even if we have to blow it to pieces in the process. These two characters war incessantly in us, and probably in most men. First one is on top, then the other — body and soul always ravaged by the internal slugging match." That is more than a self-portrait; it is a reflection of every one of us at odds with an atomic age.

Mr. White divides his time, as most of us are obliged to, between the city and the country; he hibernates in a New York apartment, in the *New Yorker's* office, and in the zoo; in the open months he lives as a farmer, a keeper of chickens and pigs on a salt-water farm in Blue Hills, Maine. It is the moralist in Mr. White that prompts him to take Senator McCarthy to Walden Pond to run down that subversive, Thoreau, and in that memorable essay he really takes the Senator for a ride. He can write just as warmly about an American boy — himself — at his first tea dance, or about Dorothy Lamour, or the death of a pig, or how it feels to be tucked away in a Boston hospital the night before an operation. The subject he loves best is America. His mood is one of compassion tinged with anger, and his humor touches your nerve.

Have we had writers in our time who have handled the essay with the high seriousness and objectivity of Francis Bacon? The answer is emphatically yes. T. S. Eliot's superb essay on "Poetry and Drama" which the *Atlantic* published in February, 1952, an essay written in memory of that beloved Harvard professor, Theodore Spencer, is one such. Another is that extraordinary definition of "Law and Manners" which Lord Moulton delivered on his retirement from the Bench. He had been a judge — a noted judge — a great parliamentarian and administrator; and at the close of his career and in a flash of insight, he examines what he calls the three great domains of human action.

"First," he says, "comes the domain of positive law, where our actions are prescribed by laws which must be obeyed. Next comes the domain of free choice, which includes all those actions as to which we claim and enjoy complete freedom. But between these two there is a third large and important domain in which there rules neither positive law nor absolute freedom. . . . It grades from a consciousness of a duty nearly as strong as positive law to a feeling that the matter is all but a question of personal choice. Some might wish to parcel out this domain into separate countries, calling one, for instance, the domain of duty, another the domain of public spirit, another the domain of good form; but I prefer to look at it as all one domain, for it has one and the same characteristic throughout — it is the domain of Obedience to the Unenforceable. The obedience is the obedience of a man to that which he cannot be forced to obey. He is the enforcer of the law upon himself."

Lord Moulton concludes: "I am not afraid to trust people — my fear is that people will not see that trust is being reposed in them . . . The great principle of obedience to the unenforceable is no mere ideal, but in some form or other it is strong in the hearts of all except the most depraved."

I believe wholeheartedly in the essay. I believe in it because it attacks complacency. I believe in it because it is lyrical in its love of nature. I believe in it because it enriches biography; because it enhances the creative process; because it respects the dignity of man. I believe in it because of its God-given laughter and above all because of its spiritual quality. The essay is not alone the possession of a professional writer as a novel is. The essay is available to and can be used by a scientist, by a busy surgeon, by a minister, by a poet, or by any amateur who chooses to write. It is the first and most congenial medium for young writers. I believe in it because it holds fast to the simple verities.

We who bear the strain of a cold war which has already lasted for nine years, and might outlast the century, can hardly believe that life will ever again be as trustful as it was when Rupert Brooke wrote his evocative poem, "The Great Lover," back in 1911. Exasperation, suspicion, and dread close in on us and take the joy out of daily living. Yet integrity and trust in this country are still at large, and that kindliness which so many foreigners have remarked as our first virtue. Perhaps the time has come to remind ourselves of what we hold dear.

III
Abroad

20

Local Color

THE clerk who was filling out my passport looked at me and asked, "Color of eyes?" "Gray," I said. "Nose?" "Long?" I suggested. "No," he said, "Roman." Lord, I thought, a Roman nose like Caesar's! To a boy who had been called "Beakstein" straight through school and freshman year because of the length of his beak, it was something to hear that he had a Roman nose.

But even with that Roman nose I could not look happy in my shirts. I had volunteered as an ambulance driver with the French Army; my pay was to be a sou a day, and I was to supply my own uniform. There was some hurry, so my father had his shirtmaker rush me half a dozen Army blouses of khaki flannel. The shirtmaker, who went on a bender once a month, was a little dim at this period and made them to my father's measurements. My collar was size 14, Father's 15½; when the shirts arrived you could have thrust your wrist down between the collar and my Adam's apple, and as for the tails — they reached to my knees. There they were, six of them, and there wasn't time to make them over.

No volunteer (I was just nineteen) ever felt more gawky than I as I went up the gangplank of the S.S. *Espagne* that

June day in 1917. She was a French liner, crowded and keyed to excitement — British and French officers, pilots of the Lafayette Escadrille, three sections of the Field Service, and two Field Hospitals complete with nurses. I inspected my stateroom, a stuffy little closet four decks down, found that I had drawn as my roommate an ex-Harvard oarsman named "Greg" Wiggins (who was soon to save my life), and with him returned to the deck.

After we passed the Statue of Liberty I went down for an early supper, and looking through the port at the sunset I had the sensation that we were rising and falling. The vibration also seemed to discourage my appetite, and after yawning fifteen times, I retired. We won't go into details, but late the following afternoon Wiggins came to my rescue with a quart of champagne and two glasses; he propped me up, made me drink my half, and helped the ghost of me into my clothes and up on deck. So I came back to life.

On my return trip in June, 1919, I was not nearly so vulnerable. Fifteen days from Saint-Nazaire to Hoboken on an Army transport . . . We slept in canvas bunks, four layers to each deck; we took our meals in relays standing up at long trestles, and when the motion was bad it would be a race between the mess kit and the rail. I remember the long hours lying stripped in the sun, the crap games on the Army blankets, with the Kentuckians cleaning up until they each had a roll that would choke a horse; I remember the shell-shock cases in wire cages at the stern of the boat deck, and I remember how, having grown six inches and put on forty pounds, I came down the gangplank at Hoboken and passed my parents, who didn't recognize me at first glance.

I was outward bound again in the autumn of 1922, this time with a scholarship at Trinity College, Cambridge. I had to work my way over, and the easiest berth I could find was on a cattle boat. Disguised in an old suit, I arrived at the ship's office in Montreal, signed over my pay to the foreman as a bribe for getting on board, and then went back to the hotel for my luggage. The taxi deposited my steamer trunk, suitcase, and portable typewriter on the long dock and departed.

Leaning on the rail above me, watching me without comment, were a number of the Scottish crew. It was obvious to me that I needed the help of at least one of them to get my stuff aboard, so I went up the gangway and added myself to the end of the line. Silence. Finally the nearest Clydesider shifted his weight my way. "We'el," he said, in a brogue too rich to reproduce, "an' I suppose you write for the papers?" I admitted as much. "Aye. An' you'll be looking for local color?" Again it seemed easier to agree. "We'el," he said, "you'll find it and it'll all be brown."

It was lucky for us that our passage down the St. Lawrence to the Strait of Belle Isle was smooth, for there had been no time to tie up our cattle — 280 steers and 11 bulls — before we caught the tide. For two days and a half they milled around while one by one we reached for their headropes and snagged them to the stanchions. The steers did not enjoy the motion any more than I did. Their malady took the form of an ever-increasing thirstiness, and twice a day I heaved the wooden buckets out of the wooden tuns, six buckets to a beast. After three days of emptiness I began to munch on a slab of cold mutton as thick as the sole of a shoe, which I had cadged from the galley. This and coffee kept me upright until the sea air revived me. I had two other consolations: H. M. Tomlinson's superb collection of seascapes, *Old Junk,* which I read lying on the bales of hay, and on the ninth day that green and golden moment of dawn as we passed the bell buoy at the mouth of the Clyde and I saw the sheep on the distant uplands and realized that we were close to shore. And to food that would stay put. Lord, how I ate when at last I got ashore! Actually I remained in Glasgow for two full days for the sheer pleasure of eating.

21

The Push Bike

IN April, 1923, I pushed off on the longest bicycle trip I shall ever make. My friend Morley Dobson and I had mapped it for the spring vacation. He was in his second year at Cambridge University, I in my first. His love of poetry was combined with a love of height; he was intent that we should have a week of climbing in the Lake Country, and the Lake poets, Wordsworth and Coleridge, went along in our knapsack. We planned to ride the Roman roads through East Anglia to York, then into the vales and dales, and across the West Riding to our headquarters at Keswick.

The Roman roads were a joy; like a smooth straight dike pointing north, they were graded for the swinging cadence of the legions, and we too limbered our leg muscles as we rode from Cambridge to Ely, and from Ely to Lincoln. At York we spent the night the better to see the Minster, to walk the old ramparts, and to poke about the little streets and bookshops. We were living on six shillings a day — $1.50 in the currency of that time — and that meant a double bed in the Temperance hotels, the cleanest and cheapest of hostelries, and if Temperance wasn't available, then we looked for a spare room over the local bakery. Fresh bread in the early morning gives you a good send-off.

From York we headed northwest to Richmond with its great Keep overlooking the river, and the ruins of the near-by abbey, which we walked to through the woods by moonlight. After Richmond we came to the vales and dales, now pushing the bike ahead of us as we slugged up the unridable pitch, and now sweeping down the broad deserted hills. It was sheep country with rocky streams and little stone farmhouses or tiny hamlets miles apart.

Our big meal of the day was breakfast — eggs and sausage, fresh rolls, strawberry jam, and buckets of tea. We'd be on the road by eight; would slow down to look at any ancient barrow, Roman ruin, or tempting church-yard; and knocked off at noon for beer and cheese at the local pub. There the advice from the inn-keeper opened up prospects for the afternoon's ride and where to spend the night. I remember that during one day's ride in York-shire we were passed by exactly two automobiles, while we in turn passed four farm carts and one old surrey. We took in the country through our eyes and our pores, and we learned that the reward of sightseeing is in inverse ratio to the speed of the driver. Usually we covered our fifty miles by 3:30, and then it was time to find that spare room, stow our knapsacks, and stretch the legs.

At Keswick we made our headquarters in a comfort-able room over the bakery, and I shall never forget the suppers of thin sliced ham, the fragrant loaves, and the comforting tea with which the baker's wife stoked us on our return from a day on the wet and windy heights. Here

we had acquired *A Handbook of Mountain Climbing* by
Mr. Abraham, the seer of the Lake Country. We also
acquired a rope and the calked boots which we needed
for the scree or the upland slopes of Scafell, Great End,
and Helvellyn. Morley had been here before, and each
morning he guided me to a convenient farm at the base
of one of these peaks. That gave us the whole day for the
climbing, and it was a tribute to our lean condition that
the only lunch we took with us was a bar of chocolate —
chocolate, and water from one of the tarns, was our forti-
fier, but the real reward was when, panting and more
frightened than we showed, we scrambled up the last
twenty yards of crusted snow and rolled over on the crest
with the world at our feet.

On one climb we disobeyed Mr. Abraham, who had
laid down firm injunctions against following the bed of a
brook in late March or early April. But it was temptingly
easy to get our footing in the early stages, and it was not
until we had reached the upper icy face, the more treach-
erous for the film of water which coated the toeholds left
by an earlier ice picker, that we realized why Mr. Abraham
had said no. Then it was too late. The rope braced us, and
I think we did the last fifteen yards with the strength of
our fingernails. We were so winded (and terrified) when
at last we flopped over the crest, that we stayed on longer
than usual munching the chocolate and reviewing our
conquest. At this moment, up the path on the safe side
(there is always a path) came a severe retired Colonel and
his obedient terrier wife. "Did you see the pair of idiots
below you," he said indignantly, "messing about on that

ice face? Really too sickening. Wonder they weren't killed!" We said we hadn't noticed.

I made the home trip alone, Morley having decided that he wanted every last minute at the Lakes. Fountains Abbey, where I spent an incredibly lovely afternoon, gave me the eerie feeling that I had been there before in another century: I all but recognized the cell I had occupied. I rode to Hadrian's Wall; I came down through what remains of Sherwood Forest; I saw Nottingham, which holds only a very few vestiges of Robin Hood, and then I found myself pushing along through the cinders and smokestacks of industrial England, the five towns of Arnold Bennett, the midlands of H. E. Bates. How I wanted to get out of it!

I finally did at Peterborough, but by that time I had run out of cash and out of air. Both tires had developed slow leaks, and had to be blown up alternately every three miles. I was down to my last sixpence and Cambridge seemed a long, long distance in the future. So I took a gamble. With my sixpence I bought a platform pass to the Peterborough railway station; there I waited for the next train to Cambridge, on the chance that among the Peterborough passengers I would find at least one man from whom I could borrow the price of a return ticket. I found him in a Trinity don, Kitson-Clark, who, after being surprised by my predicament, happily bailed me out. We had supper that night in his rooms — mutton, wine, and *crème brûlée.* And there I told him this story.

22

Editor in Ireland

I was on my way to Dublin to have a postwar visit with Irish writers and, if I were lucky, to bring back to Boston at least one big manuscript in my briefcase. On the flight from London to Dublin I sat beside an Englishman who was going to Eire for his holidays.

We came in over the Irish Sea and began to circle the lovely green headland.

"Strange, attractive place, this," said the Englishman, "it's as if you took the City of London and dropped it in little pieces all over Ireland. A bit of it fell here and that is Limerick, a larger piece here, and that's Dublin. . . ." Needless to say, that is not the Irish view. Nor is it quite the way a Bostonian first sees this romantic land from which so many of his neighbors have come.

At the Dublin airport I was met by Mary Lavin and her husband, William Walsh. We piled into their tiny red car (seating three people in a baby Austin is like seating three people in a bathtub), and off we drove to the city. It had been raining in the morning, but now those great gray clouds for which Ireland is famous were opening to show us the blue windows of the sky and the afternoon sun. The sun seemed to touch everything with fingers of gold — the great beech trees wet and still dripping, the meadows which looked like green plush, the thatched cottages in their soft pastel shades of white, rose and buff — the whole countryside was picked out in this strong, sanctified sunlight.

Now we had reached the city. We drove up O'Connell Street with its monuments and its bullet scars of the Rebellion; we passed the great gate of Trinity College and paused for a moment at St. Patrick's, where I paid my respects to Dean Swift and Stella, who now lie buried side by side in the center aisle of the noble old church. I parked my belongings at the Shelburne, an Inn straight out of Dickens, and then we began exploring the oldest parts of the city, the Georgian courts with their fan doors and their grilled balconies. But the street which *really* caught my imagination was that stretch of cobblestone and old brick houses which follows the River Liffey to the sea. These houses look half as old as time; they are built of brick, painted every color imaginable, of all sizes and shapes, with brass name plates, and with rakish chimney pots rising against the blue sky. Here live some of the oldest and strongest characters in all Dublin.

This street took us to Dublin's number one industry — the great brewery from which comes Guinness's Stout. The Guinness plant has a whole fleet of barges gaily painted in scarlet and black, barges which transfer the barrels of stout to the freight steamers at the mouth of the river. The bargemen are dressed in reefers and sailor hats, and they wear blue sweaters with the word GUINNESS across the chest. Very trim and shipshape for a voyage which measures exactly three miles downstream and three miles back!

One of the barges, with the pyramid of casks on its deck, cut loose from the quay and started on its way to the freighter in the open harbor; the tall smokestack was pulled down on a lanyard to ease it under the bridge. We noticed a Dublin loiterer leaning on the parapet, looking out to sea, and we heard him call to the immaculate bargeman passing beneath him. "Bring us back a parrot," he shouted as you might to a skipper bound for Zanzibar. "Bring us back a parrot!" The bargee had no comparable insult available.

Dublin, as you know, has been the cradle of the great Irish writers. Some of them as they came of age rebelled against discouragement or the censorship which has troubled Dublin from time to time as it has troubled Boston. Some of them rebelled and ran away to freer pastures — George Bernard Shaw to London, James Joyce to Paris. But the majority stayed in Ireland, and as the Trouble mounted and the fight for liberation became bitterly cruel, these Dublin writers lifted their voices to tell the story of the Irish character to the world. W. B. Yeats and Synge, George Moore, Sean O'Casey, Æ, James Stephens and Lady Gregory. In the Abbey Theatre they produced plays which once seen are never forgotten, like *Juno and the Paycock, The White-Headed Boy,* and *The Playboy of the Western World.*

[141]

Abroad

If you really want to understand what has made Eire the country it is today, read a little book called *The Irish,* written by a gifted, intelligent Dubliner, Sean O'Faolain. In one hundred and forty pages he has written a creative history of the growth of the Irish mind. Listen to these glowing words in which he describes that Irish rebel, Wolfe Tone, a patriot who was fighting to unite Ireland back in the 1790's:

Rebelly Wolfe Tone was doomed to leave so little behind him, to be unclear in his ideas, to be fuddled even, to be a failure, because he chose to lock-knit himself with the common people. He was not their tutor: he was their torch, their friend, their lover. He went down into the huts and cabins and took the people to his heart. He was not telling them about their future — they had no future. He was telling them about their present — about themselves. He was their second priest. It was rebels like him whom in turn the poor have always loved with an unbreakable loyalty, made ballads about them, hung their likenesses in cheap pictures about their walls, revered as their symbols.

The man who wrote this little book about the Irish, Sean O'Faolain, fought with De Valera in the Revolution when he was just twenty. Today he is, I think, the man of all writers to watch in Dublin. Several of his books, including this volume, have for a time been banned, although in this case the censorship has sensibly been withdrawn.

Mary Lavin and her husband were now driving me to their home in County Meath. We were thirsting for a good cup of Irish tea, we were hurrying, and just as we rounded a curve — *Wham!* went our left front tire, and in ten yards more we were down with a flat. William, who had been driving, said that it embarrassed him to have anyone around when he was changing a tire, and bade us go down the road for a view of Killeen Castle, the home of the Earls of Fingal. So we walked along the Irish lane beneath the shade of the tallest beech trees I have ever seen, whose upper branches were astir with doves.

We came to an opening and paused to take in the old castle. "During the Civil War many of the old places were burned," Mary Lavin told me, "some in spite, and some because they were being used as strongholds for the Black and Tan. But Killeen survived the burnings because the then Earl of Fingal had married a valiant Irishwoman who understood her people. On the night when their nearest neighbor had been burned to the ground, word came to them that the mob was on its way to Fingal. 'Arm the men,' said the steward, but the Countess intervened. 'Your house,' she said to her husband, 'has always been open to the people of Ireland; let it be so now.' So candles were lit in every room, the chandeliers were ablaze, the doors and windows thrown open. And the destroyers never came near. Or if they came, they saw and turned away. For courage and trust will touch even an inflamed mind."

While Mary Lavin was telling me this, a car suddenly came into view. The driver was a woman who slowed down at the sight of us. It was the Countess of Fingal herself. "Don't stand there when it is time for tea," she said as she recognized Mary. "Come inside with me, and tell

[143]

William to join us as soon as the tire is changed." So I saw not only the outside but the inside of Killeen Castle, the oldest part of which was built in the year 1181. I saw the great hall rising straight to the roof, the sunny library with its wide western windows and the bookshelves two stories high, the immaculate white dining room with its lovely molding. And I had my delicious Irish tea.

There is a silver dusk in Ireland when time and the light seem to stand still. And it was in this silver light that we came at last to the River Boyne and Bective House, where the Lavins were then living. We stood on the terrace which slopes down to the Boyne, and from our little height she pointed out the landmarks.

"There is the path you will follow along the river," she said, "when you come back with your salmon rod next spring. And there," she said, pointing up to the even contour of a hill which completely dominated our valley, "there," she said, "is the Hill of Tara. You have heard of Tara? Tara is where the ancient kings of Ireland used to live. Tara today is full of ghosts and ruins and no one disturbs them, not even the farmer who owns the land. . . .

"From the height of Tara," she continued, "one can see eleven of the twenty-six counties of Ireland. It is the clearest view our island affords." And she went on to tell me of the ancient love story of Diarmait and Grainne. "Grainne," she said, "was the daughter of the king of Ireland, and she was to be married on the morrow. And just to make sure that there was to be no funny business, a special guard was set about the women's quarters. All was quiet until the morning watch in those early hours before daybreak when the Captain of the Watch, Diarmait, the redheaded, glancing toward the castle, saw the princess in the open window, and came quietly closer until she saw him. They had been in love, soft words were spoken, and in no time she was out and with him speeding towards the West Coast in his chariot. After daybreak when the elopement was discovered, the King and his hosts were aroused and there far to the West they saw the fleeing couple. They set out in pursuit. But Diarmait and Grainne were first to reach the coast, and in a little ship they sought the safety of Scotland, where they lived in happiness and disguise for eleven years," said Mary Lavin, "and then the king's hosts caught up with them and slew them as they slept." Whew, I thought, how would you like to have a history like that in your front yard!

Mary and her husband were building their new cottage in a crescent of the river land, the curving Boyne to the left and to their right a meadow which sloped up to the ruins of Bective Abbey, the ghost of a monastery built by French monks in the twelfth century. After an unsurpassed supper of Irish mutton with boiled Irish potatoes as sweet as chestnuts, and fresh vegetables, we walked over to see the Abbey under the moonlight. We groped our way with an electirc torch down to the great kitchen and marveled at the rude strong vaulting overhead. We marked where the chapel had been before the great beams gave way, and then climbed to the watchtower which looked toward the river. We stepped out on a flat floor of cement guarded by the parapets and ivory-white in the moonlight.

"What in the world is this?" I asked.

"You've heard of the dancing at the crossroads," said Mary Lavin — "and how the priests forbade it as leading to immorality? Very happy they were to think that they had broken up the practice hereabouts. But the young couples, they were the sly ones; with their own hands they laid this cement floor up here in the old ruined tower where no one would think to find them. And here they dance on nights like this."

How typical that is, I thought to myself, as we descended and walked back to our open fire: the old ruin with its hidden memories and the hot young blood. And I also thought how many an American writer would envy Mary Lavin, who has the Boyne River and the Abbey to stir her imagination when her thoughts glance up from the paper. Writing against such a background as this, it is no wonder that her short stories won the James Tate Black Memorial Prize, one of the highest awards in Great Britain.

But there is one thing more that I ought to tell you about this Irish writer as nearly as possible in the words with which she told it to me. As a very young child Mary Lavin was taken to America by her father and much of her girlhood was lived in Walpole, Massachusetts. "I came back to Ireland," she once wrote me, "when I was just old enough to be powerfully impressed with the influences of a new country, but still young enough to feel a fierce

childish resentment for the loss of what was always home
— New England. It was therefore with sharpened senses
that I came under the second great influence of my life —
my years in Bective House on the banks of the Boyne,
looking out across the plains to Tara Hill. I owe a great
debt to the woodland paths and riverbank in Bective.
Here I was always alone and always glad to be alone,
wandering with idleness and aimlessness, unaware then,
but grateful now, to think that every leaf and bud and
bird was forming images that the heart can never forget."

23
Return to Dublin

ON my return visit to Ireland I flew over in the early spring, carrying with me my salmon rod and my trout rod. To shift from Boston to Ireland in April is more than a transatlantic crossing; it is a shift from a country still brown and drowsy with winter to one which is eagerly green and studded with daffodils; it is a shift from haste to leisure; a shift from the twentieth century to the eighteenth. The first thing that strikes you on your landing at Shannon is the leisurely politeness with which the Irish live. The Customs are unflurried and good-natured as they pass your luggage through. At Limerick, where you pause for a few hours awaiting your plane to Dublin, men take time to fish for trout on the low tide of the River Shannon which runs through the town; and you, with your elbows on the parapet of the bridge, have time to watch them. The angler closest to me, in boots and a faded brown tweed overcoat with a net hanging from his shoulder, landed a good fish and I lifted my hat, thinking it a happy omen.

Then back to Cruise's Royal Hotel for a leisurely luncheon — hot, thick pea soup, thin slices of roast beef with boiled praties and the inevitable sprouts, topped off by a gooseberry tart with custard. There was no office to return to, and the plane did not leave till midafternoon, so one lingered over the meal and invented thumbnail sketches about the local characters at the neighboring tables.

To enter Dublin at dusk is to step straight into the eighteenth century. In the half-light this beautiful city, with its squares and parks, with its bridges over the Liffey and the pastel crooked houses on either shore, its Trinity College, its St. Patrick's, and its limitless chimney pots of the great mansions on Fitzwilliam Street, is a living likeness of the town Dean Swift loved.

The traffic is more rapid now that there are cars rather than carriages, but the pedestrians — granted there is a change in costume — look the same. I know of no more romantic city in Europe; but curiously enough the whole story has never been told; the story of what went on in these town houses with their spacious rooms, with as many guests as children, and with a bevy of servants sleeping under the stairs; the story of the Protestant Anglo-Irish who were just as passionately Irish as the Roman Catholics; the story of the rebels, the risings, and the restraint; the story of the wealth as it flowed in from the country. Who will tell it?

After a night's rest I went forth to buy a pair of Wellingtons — the half-boots so indispensable in the spring mud — and to consult the local outfitters, Garnetts & Keegan's, about the proper flies to tempt the salmon in the River Boyne. It was a friendly consultation, which lasted over an hour. The head man, who had been fishing the river the previous Sunday, told me that the Boyne was still in winter flood, still rising because of the March rains, and my chances were a hundred to one against raising any fish with a fly. "This is what we are spinning with," he said, trotting out a Golden Sprat and some metallic-looking baits, heavily weighted. "Best have them in your kit, even though you can't use them with your light rod." With my boots I was also sold a hat, rainproof and warm, of tan whipcord with an elastic under the chin. I cannot say it became me; neither could he. "Let's face it," he remarked; "you will never win a beauty contest in that hat!"

So then to County Meath, again to that hospitable house, Bective, standing on a high shoulder overlooking the river, with its windows facing towards the Mount of Tara. The river was way up over its banks, and as brown as consommé. Thence I was driven each morning, after my Irish bacon, to fish the pools at Slane — that lovely three-mile stretch of the Boyne belonging to the Earl of Mount Charles. I don't think I've ever seen more beautiful pools on this side of the Atlantic, and there were fish in them which kept coming to the surface, but alas! they were all on the move, few holding in any pool. All the local boys were fishing with spinning rods and wooden or metal bait, plugs weighted down by sinkers which they arced in to a depth of nine or ten feet. A total of five fish, the largest twenty-five pounds, was taken along our stretch of river on Saturday and Sunday, compared with the 170 which were killed in February and the first half of March. I, with my flies, never had a follow! But, Lord! I didn't mind, for the Irish sky had opened its windows by Sunday afternoon. The sun was pouring out, and the river, the great beeches on the green banks, the white laurel and the clumps of daffodils everywhere, made a scene that was mighty restful to the spirit.

I took my lunch with me each day and ate it with a little nip of John Jameson in a tiny boathouse on stilts at the water's edge. With my feet up on the opposite bench and my back resting against the wall, I could hear and see the river going about its business. There are gratifications in the art of not-catching: the sweet smell of salmon was in the air — indeed, it fairly exuded from the frayed jacket of my gillie — and I had had the sight if not the feel of His Majesty.

In the afternoons I was less zealous and more in tune with the Irish leisure. I changed flies and experimented, with no results. Once I hooked into a small pike, and once I must have landed my bait on the very nose of what my host called "a stale fish" — a big salmon who had been loitering in the run, showing his red belly from time to time. He took up a new position ten yards downstream, and I could almost hear him mutter. Such was the sum of my achievement, but not of my happiness.

In country and back again in town I kept asking myself, Do the Irish show signs of the tension to which we have all been subjected by the atomic age? Yes, I thought, in small ways: by a flurry of libel suits; by occasionally voicing their old-time grudge against the English; and by deploring in the public prints, as well they may, the almost unstoppable bleeding away of their young manhood. (How will Ireland ever find the work and the incentive to keep her young men from emigrating?) But for most of their hours, the Irish live in an unfretful sanctuary, leisurely in what they do, polite to strangers, hospitable to the guest — one's visit is never long enough, and throughout it one listens to the lilt and the rhythm of the Irish voice: the artificial imposition of Gaelic has not yet impaired their musical appropriation of the English language. I hope it never will.

24
Spanish Walnut

ABINGDON lies seven miles south of Oxford, and the last time that I had taken this road was in July of 1943. On that sunny afternoon, I remember that the air had been heavy with the sound of bombers being tuned up by the mechanics for the evening take-off. The farms I passed had been converted into an endless relay of airfields. The metal strips ran through the standing wheat; and the control tower commanded, among other things, the geese and chickens of the nearby farmyard. As our bus passed the entrance to the fields, we were waved at by the ground crews, and the two robin-breasted farm girls at the window in front of me got the familiar American wolf call.

On that summer's day in the war, I had come from Air Marshal Harris's headquarters, where I had been one of a party of three editors to whom the Bull, as he was nicknamed, had shown the results of the recent raids. Here were the huge photographs, before and after, brought back by the reconnaissance planes; we heard the persuasive British argument for area bombing, and we also heard for the first time the tribute to Lord Trenchard. "It was he who saw further than any of us," said the Bull. "He got us our appropriations, small though they were, and it was

[153]

he, more than any other man, who was responsible for
having our Hurricanes and Spitfires in production in that
desperate year after Munich." Those were the war thoughts
I had in mind as I took the bus from Oxford to see John
Masefield.

That was seven years ago, and now my hired car was
passing the same farms on my return to Abingdon. I
noticed a landing field that had gone back to seed. The
Nissen huts had been taken over by a squatter colony—
married veterans, many of them, who couldn't find houses
in overcrowded Oxford; the washing was hung and the
children were playing where the ground crews used to
sweat it out. Farther along I saw a hangar which had been
converted into a showroom for McCormick tractors. But
the biggest field of all, closest to Abingdon, was still in the
possession of the Fleet Air Arm; the planes with their
wings folded like grasshoppers were parked in the hangars
as they would be on a carrier, and others were being
tuned up. It was a big installation and the jet planes here
would have made Bull Harris's mouth water, I thought,
could he have had them in 1943.

Again I walked down the flint driveway with the rooks
circling and scoffing at me overhead. Again, now as then,
it was the poet himself who came to greet me at the door.
As Mrs. Masefield poured us tea, our talk turned to the
Spanish galleon — one of the Armada — which had been
sunk off the island of Mull and which divers from the
Admiralty were now trying to salvage from the mud, the
fierce currents, and the depths. "They have got her free of

the mud," said Masefield, "and if they can manage that tricky current, I think they will have her up. Here is a piece of her they sent me."

We examined the chunk, the size of a man's palm, and with my finger I traced the fan of the grain. "Oak?" I asked.

"No," he said, "I think more likely Spanish walnut. They might have had us, you know," he continued reflectively. "With that strong wind at their back the Armada was actually at the gates of Plymouth before we could do anything about it. The wind was so strong and so dead against us that our ships could not get out of harbor. They really had us at their mercy, and had they come in then as some of the younger captains wanted, there'd have been more Spanish blood in the South of England today. . . .

"But the Spanish Admiral had none of Nelson's audacity. He had no heart for this command, he didn't really want it. Also, he was under orders to pick up the Duke of Parma and load aboard his army, which was waiting on the French coast. Those Spanish ships were huge floating forts, and they were fought by soldiers. While he was doing this the wind began to shift in our favor and so our ships got out. People forget what a daring innovator Hawkins was. When it was known that the Spanish were building the Armada, Hawkins went to the Queen with plans for smaller, swifter ships. Oh, he checked with Raleigh and the other great captains; he knew what he was doing — and here was the big innovation: this little British fleet was to be manned and fought entirely by sailors! He believed that they could work the guns faster and with their better navigation they would be much more deadly in their broadsides. And so it worked out. . . .

"As the Spanish came lumbering on, beating up against the wind, it was the British ships that had the speed and the wind at their back. The Spanish ships, towering and pitching, fired right over us, and so Hawkins drove them away or sank them, just as the Hurricanes and Spitfires were to drive away those bombers of Göring's. The Spaniards had not come provisioned for adversity; and as they were driven off course by our ships and the mounting storm, they ran out of food, they suffered from thirst, and they went down on the rocky, inhospitable coast."

"How many did they lose?" I asked.

"About a hundred and fifty ships, I seem to remember — a hundred and fifty out of the two hundred that started. About fifty of them to our gunfire, and a hundred to ship- wreck and disaster.

"When they brought the news to Philip he was shocked with grief, for one of his dearest friends — and he hadn't many — had gone down with his ship. Then, as he re- covered, he said slowly, 'It is a proof of God's favor that I have the power to build a second Armada.' But of course he didn't. And of those few captains who straggled back, many never recovered; it was because of the humiliation quite as much as their long exposure. Four admirals had gone out; one came back and he went straight to bed, would neither eat nor drink, but turned his face to the wall, and there he died."

Spanish Walnut

Such was the story that little chunk of walnut called out of the poet. His cheeks flushed as he told it. Listening, it was easy to imagine what the thought of invasion has meant to this plucky, phlegmatic people. Goering and the Battle of Britain were yesterday and the Armada the day before. He gave me to see it as if he had been there on the deck.

25
A Proper Day

"ARE you here to read or are you here for pleasure?" is the first question put to an American editor when he arrives in London, and if your answer is yes to both, as mine was, within forty-eight hours all shelf space in your sitting room and bedroom, all table tops, and most chairs will be piled high with manuscripts, bound proofs, and advance copies of English publications hoping for acceptance in the United States. It is agreeable to have a wife along to share the eyework with you (mine was), and it is imperative to find a competent English secretary who will not be baffled by American idiom and who will keep sending the undesirable candidates back to their points of origin. English literary agents and publishers are punctilious, and it would never do to return a manuscript to the wrong sanctum. As in times past, I was saved from this embarrassment by Pat Brayne, a cheery, impeccable secretary.

The day began at 8:30 with breakfast served in our sitting room. Since there is no good orange juice in the United Kingdom and since every American in the first week feels puffed up by the starchy diet, we bought fresh oranges and clusters of rich purple grapes from the barrows on Piccadilly. Editorial ideas are stimulated by food and drink, and I not infrequently have breakfast engagements when in New York or Washington; but abroad I kept this hour for private cogitation since the London schedule (a word they always mispronounce) provides five other occasions when an editor can entertain or be entertained by his clientele: luncheon, tea, "drinks" (our cocktail hour), dinner, and supper (from 10 P.M. on). Having confirmed the day's engagements in my little black book, I settled down to a quiet morning with the Great Brayne.

On my very first visit to an agent's office I acquired two unpublished manuscripts by Dylan Thomas; the rich and perceptive short stories by Wolf Mankowitz came next, and good things after that until I had bought more than a score of contributions for the magazine — and still the quest went on. For new fiction I turned to old friends, Geoffrey Household, Mollie Panter-Downes, H. E. Bates and Enid Bagnold. Richard Gordon, whose books, *Doctor in the House* and *Doctor at Sea,* have sold three quarters of a million copies in England, agreed to look into the several years of research the Harvard Hospital outside of Oxford has devoted to the Common Cold (and how you don't get it). A golf tournament was being played in a high wind with hard, fast greens, and the anguish as reported by the *Times* prompted me to write to Bernard Darwin for a paper on "Golf in the High Wind."

With the sun flooding Half Moon Street (we had twenty-six days of sunshine) and with Piccadilly and Green Park only half a block from my windows, it was tantalizing to think of the London that would beckon if one were not bound to print. Occasionally in the afternoons I rebelled. I sauntered down St. James's to buy a hat in Lock's; pored over salmon flies at that beloved shop, Hardy's Fishing; saw the exhibition of portraits by Augustus John; or I went window-shopping in the Burlington Arcade, where I bought a half-dozen neckties, sniffed my way through that most fragrant and tasteful emporium, Fortnum & Mason, or with the help of Mr. Forester of Leader's ticket agency made my reservations for the shows that were hard to get into: *Airs on a Shoe-string, The Boy Friend,* and that slice of English Chekhov, *A Day by the Sea,* in which Sir John Gielgud and Sir Ralph Richardson led an incomparable cast.

The food in London is to my liking. The lobster, grilled Dover sole, and poached turbot (Nelson's favorite fish) as served at the Mermaiden, an appendage of Fleming's, are memorable. The sirloin steak at Isow's, in Soho, and the beefsteak and kidney pie at the Ivy, where the literati gather, the juicy duck I had at the Caprice (the hardest of all to get into — be sure you telephone in advance), the hors d'oeuvres and mutton at the Ritz — these were some of the "bests" I enjoyed.

The number of good restaurants has multiplied and one can't hope to cover them all in three weeks; I brought back with me as an appetizer for future visits that succulent and amusing booklet, *London Night and Day,* illustrated by Osbert Lancaster. Mr. Lancaster is one of those versatile gents for whom there is no simple label: artist and architect, a cartoonist whose comics in the

Beaverbrook press are as popular as anything in *Punch,* a connoisseur and a lover of Greece, he is that rarity, a contemporary historian who can capture the façade of an age and the habits and quiddities of those who lived in it. His memoirs of his Victorian childhood, *All Done from Memory,* which has been published with us though not yet in England, provides a perfect reminder for Americans viewing London from the outside.

Now I had a week end at Oxford coming up; and since one's time there is never long enough, I telephoned ahead to make sure that my friends were free. On May Day, the Saturday of our arrival, Sir Richard Livingstone took us in tow and a better educator or more kindly humanist does not exist. With him we drove out to Boar's Hill to pay our respects to Gilbert Murray, the classicist who has done more to retrieve the beauty of the Greek plays than any other man in our time. Mr. Murray, then in his eighty-ninth year, had been invited that spring to deliver the annual address before the Classical Association, and the words he spoke on the theme "Are Our Pearls Real?" were received with a standing ovation. When we left his book-lined study with its pleasant view of the sloping garden and the fruit trees in bloom, I had his promise that he would send me a copy.

That afternoon we motored out to have tea with John Masefield at Burcote Brook, and once again I came under the spell of that deep voice as he spoke of English history in a way that made us feel that it happened only yesterday. I asked if he would show me again the fragment of the

Armada that the English divers had sent him from the treasure ship sunk in the channel off the Isle of Mull; this led to his telling of the scandalous sinking of the *Royal George,* a minute-by-minute account — the poet said he was paraphrasing David — which made the tilting deck and the panic as she split seem as graphic as the *Lusitania.*

Sunday I was introduced to All Souls by Isaiah Berlin, and there at supper met the younger dons and Maurice Bowrer, the Vice-Chancellor. One other Cambridge man besides myself was present, Noel Annan, a Fellow of King's, and he and I did our best to hold the bridge against the banter and badinage which Oxford loves to heap upon the Light Blue.

Which brings me to an observation first begun thirty years ago: that English conversation has a probing, a mimicry, a rude and teasing sting which is the perfection of small talk and which, when they are working on one another, reduces the visitor to silence — he can't compete. They epitomize, deprecate, laugh at, and satirize their opposite numbers with devastating wit. Whistler I think of as one American who acquired the art, and an art it is. To listen to the two country squires, Evelyn Waugh, the novelist, and Cyril Connolly, the critic, deploring their boredom away from London; or Humphrey Ellis tell of his dinner on a Spanish train, or Kenneth Tynan, their best dramatic critic, compare the mores of Broadway with those of the London theater, is to be convulsed.

And this in turn leads to a remark on their reading. English readers follow their proclivity far more widely

than we. They are captivated by no list of best sellers
(none is printed), and the book clubs corral only a frac-
tion. Travel books (Spain and Africa seem in the ascend-
ency today), religious books, books on gardening, yacht-
ing, mountain climbing, prehistoric Britain, Buddhism,
and modern architecture, all have their loyal following.
The English are undimmed by any infatuation with television. Difficulties of style do not stand in the way of their
enjoying a gifted writer like Ivy Compton-Burnett, who
is seldom read on our side. They read.

And so back to my little suite on Half Moon Street,
where Shelley had once lived, back to more books, correspondence, and manuscripts, back to the climax of the
trip and what might be termed "a proper English day."
My dear old mountaineer, Morley Dobson, the poet, had
come down from the Lake Country and we held a twenty-
year reunion beginning with fish and chips at the Mermaiden. We made reservations for *Twelfth Night* at the
Old Vic, and then headed down to the riverbank to spend
the afternoon at the Tower of London.

This visit to the Tower was something neither would
have done without the other, but five minutes after we had
surrendered ourselves to the guidance of our Beefeater, I
am sure we were both happy we had come. It is a cruel
and bloody scroll of the British past which unrolls for
you as you cross over the drawbridge and move from
tower to tower. But the plaintive records make the gray
pile live: the Biblical texts scratched into the stone by
prisoners during their long vigil; the rampart where Elizabeth, the girl, took her daily walk never knowing whether

[163]

Queen Mary would that week order her execution; the tower where Sir Walter Raleigh was caged for twelve years before he was beheaded; the instruments of torture, the hook, thumbscrews and manacles; the chopping block, the giant ravens, the ancient gleaming armor, and St. John's Chapel in the White Tower, with its Norman beauty and the brass plate on the wall telling of its blazing past. "No more bloodthirsty than our own time," remarked Morley as at last we re-emerged into the twentieth century.

While Morley and my wife had tea, I changed into a dark suit and was whisked off to the House of Commons to see the Prime Minister. Sir Winston, pink-skinned, clear-eyed, made me welcome with a spot of Scotch and a long cigar, and the brief absorbing visit that followed I shall long remember. I had brought him page-proofs of our leading article, "Churchill Was Right" by Hanson Baldwin, and the examination led him to speak of earlier, momentous decisions reaching back to the Kaiser's threat at Agadir. When at last the Bobby escorted me to my cab I was ready for roast beef and Shakespeare — a proper ending for a proper English day.

IV
The North Woods

26

Delicate Bamboo

BECAUSE I find fishing, the play of sunlight and shadow on water and the signals of the life beneath, the most complete and bewitching relaxation from a life devoted to print, I am occasionally asked for advice, not as an expert but as an addict who has learned from his trials. "Jack has always had a yen to fish," said the wife of a friend recently, "but now that he's got the time, he's too shy to begin. Claims he doesn't know anything about casting or what tackle to get. How do I push him in?" I think that's true of more fifty-year-olds than ever admit it: their friends who belong to the fraternity of the dry fly talk a jargon that will scare away most beginners. What Jack needs for his conversion is the joy of catching fish; the art of not catching he can develop later. Specifically, what he needs is an old hat, a pair of sneakers, and a bottle of insect repellent. I did my learning on a Bristol split-bamboo rod that cost sixteen dollars; Jack can do his on a medium-priced fly rod and reel at a cost of thirty dollars, or as much more as he cares to pay (the famous-name rods, a Leonard, a Thomas, a Paine, or a Hardy, will come close to one hundred dollars.)

But most of all, Jack needs the tight line and the feel

of a jumping smallmouthed or the swift rush of a trout. He should not be ashamed to use bait. I know two friends who fish a mountain brook. The brook has two branches winding through three miles of thick brush. They leave one car at the bottom, drive to the top, and go their separate ways with worm cans. They never fail to catch enough brookies for the meal when they converge — and incidentally, the bottom pool is an excellent icebox for their bottled beer. So what Jack needs is worms for the trout brook, or minnows or hellgrammites for the bass pond. Plenty of time for the dry flies after his conversion.

A second friend, setting off in early July for a month's cruise which will carry him as far as Newfoundland, asked if I thought he could hold a salmon on his telescopic steel rod. I said I thought he could, and gave him the names of the three standard wet flies (Size 4) which a salmon might rise to at the river's mouth — the Black Dose, Durham Ranger, and Mar Lodge. That collapsible steel rod of his is probably the best all-purpose implement for one who will be fishing as opportunity permits, in the sea, river mouth, or fresh water — and who won't take much time cleaning up his gear. I have seen one of these steel rods bring in thirty tinker mackerel by trolling pork rind through the schools over which the terns work so beautifully; I have seen it land an eight-pound striper which struck at a Mickey Finn. I have seen it cranking in flounders and cod; and though I have never seen it kill a salmon, I believe it could if the line and backing were strong enough.

My third query comes from the parents of a ten-year-old. The boy will be spending this summer on an island off the coast of Maine, but he will be fishing inland later, and they want something for both. In this case I am inclined to recommend a glass rod 8 or 9 feet in length, weighing 4½ to 6 ounces, with an extra tip. (The rod and reel should not cost more than twelve dollars.) Most of his fun will be still-fishing, using a bobber or depending upon that telegraphic tug, and I'd rather see him get used to a long rod than a short bait caster, which is a specialty. A glass rod will weather the difference between salt water and fresh without rusting, and the tip is not so likely to be "set" (that is, be bent) by that fierce pull when you think you have hooked a monster and only have the bottom. But for the boy whose initiation will begin on the fresh-water stream or lake, I still favor the split bamboo, because to me it is more responsive than either steel or glass, and because it has a beauty which a boy who may be sloppy in other respects will treasure. Steel looks indestructible, so you leave it around; glass can't be broken, so you don't worry; bamboo you know is fragile, so you varnish and wipe it and sleep with it.

Even the vigilant are sometimes betrayed. Three of us were paddling home this June after some evening fishing on the Ipswich River; the sun had gone down, and we were working hard against the strong current, cutting a diagonal between the maples and alders which reached across from either bank. I yelled to my son, Ted, to pick it up, and dug hard with my own paddle; as he finished his stroke he turned back and, hearing him gasp, I looked around just in time to see my lovely Thomas rod lifted out of the stern by a grasping maple branch and deposited full length and without a trace in seven feet of water. It was too dark to do anything more than mark the spot, and we went home. I was too morose to be cheered. Before ten the next morning — it had come on to rain — Ted and I, with Fritzy to cheer us, paddled back to the same spot, now in our bathing suits, and it was raw cold. We had borrowed a pair of rubber swim fins; and with these to help us in our swimming against the current, we dove and searched the bottom. Ted was sure the rod must have drifted at least fifteen feet downstream from where it fell, so he explored in that area. The current would drive him back ten yards and he came up sputtering beside the canoe. I began my diving a little ahead of the point where I had last seen the rod disappear, knowing the current was so strong that I'd be washed back before I reached the sand floor. Six times in succession I kicked down, scraping my nose on the sightless bottom, and grappling for water-logged branches, for pebbles, or nothing; and then in one last desperate reach I touched the smooth, delicate tip of the rod, and light as a feather it lifted as I thrust it up toward the surface. Of all those square inches of sandy bottom, how did I touch that one? What luck!

27
Kennebago

THE fever of games is very contagious in this country. I notice that those who were not cut out to be athletes in college sometimes have a delayed attack of competition in later life. But latent in most of us, especially those who are suburbia bred, is the desire to know the country — to identify ourselves with the streams, the mountains, and the sea — and so in midlife, as the zest for tennis or golf plays itself out and subsides, we hear a new call, a call to do things in the open with our children — camping, fishing, cruising, hunting with guns or camera, the reaching out for unspoiled America and for shared experience which brings alive the antennae we had almost forgotten we possessed.

I had not realized this was happening to me until some years ago on a winter night an older man (he had just lost his only son of college age) and I were walking home toward Beacon Hill, talking of fishing as we breasted the snowstorm. I remarked unguardedly that I enjoyed fishing with young Ted. "Do it," he said, and I felt the emotion in his voice. "Do it every chance you get! You have him with you for so short a time."

The admonition comes back to me across the years; now

that old Bob himself is dead, I know the urgency he felt: the war years, the insecurity, the military training ahead, have intensified the same desire in hundreds of thousands of other families, as I noticed after the war from the cars heading north with canoe racks, trailers, dogs at the open window, and the youngsters piled in with the duffel in the back seat.

Our log cabin in the Rangeley country faced north to the Blue Mountains, the Kennebago Range, and the almost three hundred miles of wilderness stretching between our lake and Quebec; off to the right was the mountain trail taken by Benedict Arnold and his "rabble in arms" on that march Kenneth Roberts has depicted so magnificently in his novel; to the left the peak at the end of the lake had the fire ranger's lookout like a tiny saltcellar at its very tip. The green heights and valleys receding in the distance caught the sunset in different planes of light and shadow; the deep water off our float was glassy but dimpled where a fish rose, and from down the lake we heard the mockery of the loon. This was our first impression.

In the seven days that followed, dawn and dusk took on a new meaning. The kingfishers blustered at us in our early exploration of the lake. Black duck and the goldeneye whistlers rose as our boat probed the lagoon of the Boneyard, where the great gray skeletons of the trees traced the forest that was, before the lumberman cut and flooded the land. Sheer white against the spruce were a pair of egrets — the first, the natives told us, ever to venture this far north. The little sandpipers pecked and scurried along the sandy shore, and always we were on the lookout for those silent marauders, the hawks and the young eagle.

We fished as a family, our three rods always busy; and with Jim O'Brien, our guide and the best cook in Maine, we took as many meals as possible on the river and lake shore. I remember his trout chowder — onions, thin-sliced potatoes, and a dozen small trout skinned, boned and delectable as they were brewed in the milk. Trout chowder, toast, crisp bacon, blueberries, spice cake and coffee, and then a nap stretched out under the balsam. The pink-fleshed trout of the stream are a delicacy no restaurant provides. They were our staple and we topped them off with wild raspberries or blueberries which we gathered as Jim made the fire.

I know now better than ever before the restraint and rivalry, the teasing and the pride, which are all a part of family fishing. Young Ted of course would never leave the water alone. Casting from the float at the end of the first day he derricked in a nine-and-a-half-incher (exact by tape measure) and then came running to report, "Boy, he sure would have put up a fight if I hadn't caught him on the backcast!"

We all learned from Jim, and Ted learned the most. The skill, the discipline so shrewdly conveyed in the boat and on the stream, the quiet teasing as when Jim took over the youngster's line, straightened out the snarls in the leader, made a single cast, hooked into a good fish,

turning the rod back to Ted with the remark, "Look what
you had on your line, son — why didn't you pull him up?";
the pride felt but unexpressed when the thirteen-year-old
skunked us all by netting two salmon under his mentor's
eye; the walk home under the moonlight, the boots clumping, and the note of triumph creeping into each individual's recital.

Good guides are quiet-spoken, and the example is
soothing to city nerves. There is plenty of exasperation in
fishing, and when I had been fighting my dry fly in a
perverse wind one hot afternoon, tangling the brown puff
in my rod every third cast, it took a quiet remark of Jim's
to blow my head of steam.

"River's full of fish," he said, "and you'll get one if you
rest the pool. Might even get that six-pounder that's got
so many hooks in him that they wanted him for the
scrap drive."

Jim's gravity was forever fooling us: he spoke so seriously that we were never prepared. "Want to hear me call
a moose?" he asked one twilight as we were trudging
towards home. We stopped. He scanned the horizon, fixed
his eyes on a distant point, cupped his lips, took a prodigious breath, and said, "Here, moosey, moosey, moosey."
Coming from a two-hundred-and-thirty-pounder, it was
wonderfully silly.

Another time he had been telling us about the great
forest fires of last year. "They were bad," he said, "real
bad." A pause. "Did you hear about the herd of deer up
here got caught with smoke and cinders in their eyes?
Blinded. But there was one young buck who could see:

he lined them up and led six of them across the river each holding on to the other's tail. But a guide crept up, cut the buck's tail, led the does into camp, and had himself enough deer meat to last all winter."

28

Nova Scotia

ON a family expedition, it's the little things that count. As we hummed north on the Maine toll road to Portland, a huge duck hawk zoomed up from the brook where he'd been feeding beneath the level of the road. We were doing sixty — so, for an instant, was he — and as he hung there with his beautiful wingspread and the crescent of his tail feathers less than a foot from our side window, it was breathtaking whether we'd collide. Then he swerved into the trees.

Later that afternoon, in the Maine uplands, in the yard of one of those blue-gray, long-unpainted farmhouses, we caught a glimpse of a wrestling match: the farmer with his pitchfork trying to uproot the porcupine, and Porky bristling fiercely as he tried to retreat to his cellar hole.

We have been over this road before, and the landmarks — the glass hearse in the yard of an antique seller, Perry's Nut House (where we always take food aboard), and the house with the captain's walk in Camden — are old friends.

There are family jokes which we carry on as we drive. A family joke, unlike most others, gains on repetition. I, for instance, am on the lookout for a place of retirement when I've earned enough scars from editing. "Well, there it is, at last," I say as we pass over a blue, fast trout stream, with an abandoned farm on the knoll above. "That's my place. 'Boats for Rent, Bait for Sale, Try Week's Trout Chowder.'" "Haven't you had enough of New England winters by this time?" asks Fritzy. "Don't be silly. You can sell bait just as effectively in Virginia." Young Ted, on the other hand, has his eye on the little motels and diners and he keeps a tally of the fancier names: "Chick-Inn," "Sail Inn," "Better Duck Inn." "When we have ours," he remarks, "we'll call it 'Auto-Stop-Here.'"

In the woods we make a conscious effort to share the burdens — and the pools. Every city-pent angler yearns for the first cast over unfished water, but when there are three rods to take turns — father, mother, and son — the predatory is disciplined by the parental instinct. Our fishing is best when the competition is tempered by affection, for it is *almost* as much fun to watch one of the family net a good fish as to net it yourself. In this delicate adjustment it is John, the Nova Scotian, who decides. He has fished these pools for fifty years, he has known them when the trout were larger and more plentiful, but his faith is undiminished. "You've whaled that pool long enough," he decides. "If there was a trout there, he'd have shown long before this. They ought to be dancing on their tails this early in the morning. Now you take Charlie's Pool and we'll try the Outlet." Thus he rouses anticipation as we wait our turn. So, too, at the portages John's resourcefulness at seventy calls out the voluntary spirit in his juniors and there is no argument about sharing the pack, the pots, the ponchos, and the gear as we file through the woods.

For the second year in succession the Lady present has caught the biggest fish. Last year of course it was just luck — we haven't too much respect for her casting — but this time what happened at Thomas Pool can't be laughed off. Luncheon was over; the fried trout, the big slabs of homemade bread toasted over the embers, the canned peaches, and John's thick black coffee — "That coffee really is able!" John remarks as he passes the enameled cups — had reduced Ted and me to the horizontal. We lay on our backs, resting those shoulder muscles unused to so much paddling. John leaned back against a tree, lit a cigarette, and sighed. "Well," he said, "if I had a farm I'd sell it and go guiding." Out of the corner of our eyes we saw Ma take the light rod and head down the piney corridor toward the pool, unruffled in the bright sun. "Watch your backcast," I murmured. Poor Ma, with those overhanging trees, she'd be lucky to get out fifteen feet, the leader and line all splashing down with a galump. The sun was blazing overhead; it was too bright. Our smoke was broken by a shout that meant business; and as we ran, there, framed in bright light, was the picture — the bowed rod throbbing to the down pull, the big square tail and the black back breaking water. John launched her in the canoe and the fight went on in the center of the pool. Ted and I shook hands when at last Gargantua, a two-and-a-half-pound brook trout, had been netted; but it wasn't until that night that he expressed himself. "I didn't congratulate you on your fish this after-noon," he said to his mother as he climbed into his blankets. "But I meant to. He's a great fish. Only, Ma, I wish you wouldn't always try to catch the biggest one; it makes it tough for me when the boys ask who got the big one!"

Candor and consolation — the Lady contributes both. As on the following day when, having caught my favorite blue fly in a high branch, I elected to mount from the canoe to a steep rock from which I hoped to tip down the branch. To reach the rock I had to edge in over the birch branches of a beaver house, a fussy business which made me impatient. As I got a firm footing with one sneaker on the rock, all unconsciously I thrust away with my retaining foot in the canoe. The further the canoe retreated the further I stretched until, rather than split, I lunged into the water and scrabbled for the rock. No word was spoken until I had salvaged the fly. Then: "With all that commotion," remarked the Lady, "you shook down a dozen caterpillars. I wonder if a trout would take one?" My wetness, stupidity, and barked knee were forgotten in the new possibility. She handed me one of the gray, silky, blue-lined caterpillars, and from the tip of my paddle I dropped it in the run. It drifted twenty feet; there was a sudden snack and it was gone. The little things that count . . .

29
To the Northwest Miramichi

WE always pack too late and rise too early; yawning and with the fever of anticipation in our blood we set out on the road which takes us north for our July sojourn in the New Brunswick forest. The road is crowded at first with holiday seekers like ourselves, the cars loaded with children, bedding, and cameras, radios blaring, and a spaniel muzzling the wind. We leave behind us the white spires of Newburyport, Portsmouth harbor seen from the bridge over the Piscataqua, and the Kittery Navy Yard. In no time, the Maine toll road speeds us on our way to Portland, and its woody stretches alert our city senses for the wilderness ahead. We slow down for Brunswick, that lovely college town with its Bowdoin pines — what it must have been like when they hemmed it in! — and then we enter the long avenue of resorts: Wiscasset, Damariscotta, Rockland, Camden, Searsport, with the stately white homes of the sea captains such a calm backdrop for the gaudy slacks and halters of the summer visitors. Could the skippers return, which do you think they would find the odder, the fannies or the dark glasses? This is a Gluyas Williams comedy and we are part of it as we pass.

North of Lincoln the traffic has dispersed, and we are

alone on the spruce-pointed road whose winter heaves and billows are made tolerable only by the occasional glimpse of wild life; a porcupine enjoying his brookside salad, his rear quills a warning to wayfarers; a red-tailed hawk startled by our approach; and always the deer — half-grown does, mostly, and as unpredictable as cattle in their sudden preference for the other side of the road. Like Mr. Milquetoast we slow down for those signs which say DEER CROSSING.

We approach the Border at Vanceboro — and now we're in Canada, and it's another country with its different colors and emblems, its frank civility, and — I hate to say this — with its much more evident respect for land and law. You see no such roadside litter as ours once you cross the border; the graveyards of dead automobiles which deface so many of our communities are inconspicuous (these maritime people have less to do with), and the rivers are blue and unpolluted. The corruption of our famous American streams is an inevitable result of wealth and progress, but I do wish the States would give recognition to those counties which begin to clean up what industry and town sewerage have poisoned. Maine has made a beginning: the salmon have come back to the Dennys and the Narraguagus, and there is talk of depollution and a fish ladder for the Aroostook; but the Kennebec, the Penobscot, and the Bangor Pool, lovely as they still are to the eye, long ago lost their underwater vitality because of industrial waste — most damaging of all, the lignin of the paper mills.

It is not easy to protect a river or a forest, and Canadians when they go on the warpath can be just as wanton as any American. I have in mind one thirty-mile stretch of New Brunswick forest which was cut, bulldozed, and ravaged in the 1950's — the rape was supervised by an expert forester, condoned by a great paper company, and afterwards mildly censured by the Province. I wish more Canadians could see this devastation, for it is a sight that makes you cry out in indignation. It is, of course, an exceptional case, but it shows how far the greed for dividends can go north of the Border.

The river of our heart, the Northwest Miramichi, lies more than a hundred miles north of Fredericton and the approach to it is something to dream of on a winter's train. At Boiestown, we coast down into the valley of its big cousin, the broad Southwest Miramichi, and into pleasant memories of Jack Russell's famous camp; of Bliss Perry and the dawns and dusks he describes at Burnt Hill; and of the Half Moon trip — a fifty-mile canoe run downstream, fishing and camping as you go — which still can be arranged if you say the right word to the right man, Clayton Stewart. (The canoes are loaded aboard the evening train out of Boiestown.) Then comes Doaktown where Wallace Doak ties the most captivating flies for this watershed — look for his leaping salmon sign on the left-hand side of the village street; and so to Newcastle, where we turn sharp left and head for Trout Brook and the Gatehouse, where we must register before entering the forest. Frank, who has welcomed us before, gives us the news and we compliment him on the four-hundred-pound bear whose hide is stretched on the shed. Frank's wife keeps their log cabin as neat as fresh scrubbed wood can be, and it is a standing joke between us that we shall move in here when we retire.

Ever a light sleeper I become more sensitive than usual to the night sounds when we unpack in our camp beside the running water. Dam Camp, where we spend the first half of our stay, is poised box-square on a rocky bluff looking down upon a fourteen-foot falls and the Corner Pool below it. The white water comes over with the force of a fire hose, and the sound of it is always in your ears, not a murmur but a rushing. On the porch which girdles the cabin, you can stand at day's end, watching the beautiful dark arrows of the salmon as they leap the falls in the twilight. They are halfway, seven feet in the air, before you know it; and if their aim is perfect they hit the very center of the dashing water where it bulges outward over a rocky shelf; here for a moment they are silhouetted, then a second vibrating spring which seems to shake the whole fish lifts him over the top and that big square tail disappears into the still water beyond the lip. To leap from the depths with such power and accuracy is their nature, and a wonder they have performed again and again in their hundred-mile journey upstream. But if they miss the center point, the falls hurl them aside and they hit the rocks with a solid smack before dropping back into the pool. The rocks to either side are covered with fish scales and as slippery as velvet.

In this spot an exclamation from my boyhood comes back to me —"Great Day in the Morning!" we used to shout at each other on the Jersey Coast when the sea air

and sunlight made us feel that we were on top of the
world. And now again my blood quickens at the urging
of a Great Day in the Morning. Perhaps it is why sleep
comes so lightly. The evening fishing is over a half-hour
after sunset, and we are dog-tired as we trail back to
camp; I have juice enough left to banter with Howard, our
head guide, as I pull out the silk line to dry, or jot down
some notes in the log, but by eleven I am out like a
light. What is it, then, that calls me back into instant
being as early as three-thirty or four? It could be the
drumming of rain on the shingles, or the high, far note
of the white-throated sparrow, or the sound of the falls,
but more persistently I think it is anticipation, anticipation of the day ahead. I have drifted off to sleep planning
exactly what I shall do when my turn comes to fish the
Ledges or Mountain Brook and suddenly I am called to
the wings, waiting for the curtain to rise.

It is an olive-green world I step into, quietly, not letting
the screen door slam. In the pre-dawn the cold mist hangs
like a diminutive fog bank close to the water. Until it
disperses and the sunrise gives me perspective, I cannot
see a moving fish or the waving shadows which tell
where they lie; what I can see are the deer as they come
down to drink — more often a doe and her fawn; once
and unforgettably, against the evergreens, the red russet
saddles of a buck and two does seen just as the sun's
finger fell on them.

The path down the bluff to Corner Pool is heavy with
dew and slippery — I'll get sopped if I skid; I go down
gingerly and out to the shingle, where I crouch behind

the protecting bush. The pool is forty yards across and it shelves sharply to a depth of twenty feet. Through the multiple panes of water which are racing by, through the foam and bubbles, I occasionally get a clear glimpse of the concourse of salmon and grilse, a procession heading toward the base of the falls and ceaselessly circling. They will not leap in as much light as this, nor will they rise to the fly as long as they are in that procession. Their size and number make me shiver. Are there fish like this in the other pools?

This is too good to miss. The sky is cloudless and it will probably be blazing hot by eleven; my watch says it is five-thirty — and I think it's time Jimmie got up, so I climb the rocky path to camp and go to the cot where he is slumbering. "Jim," I whisper, shaking his shoulder — "Jim, it's a cool morning and Corner's alive with fish. Get up!"

He struggles to the surface and fixes me with a bleary eye. "What time is it?"

"Nearly six."

"Weeksie," he says thickly, "you're biling the kittle at both ends. Go back to bed." And his head snuggles down.

Resigned, I go out back to the cookhouse where I know that Howard will be stirring. I have been here before at this hour and once, appearing silently on the river path by the back door, caught a basin full of hot water square in the face, tossed out as Howard finished his shave. "Man, I didn't know you were there," he cried, before we broke into laughter. So now I call ahead of me: "Watch out for the hot water!"

[185   ]

The North Woods

Cook is getting the guides' breakfast and the kitchen is warm and fragrant with the frying bacon, the coffee, and the hotcakes. I have brought with me a box of my bedraggled dry flies: mounting them one at a time on a matchstick, I hold them up to the spout of the kettle to let the steam freshen and frizzle their wings. Then, with my pitcher of hot water, I make for the washhouse to shave.

I shall have had three hours of morning and a breakfast as hearty as the guides before I make my first cast for a fish. The pools, which we draw by lot, will give each angler plenty of water to cover before noon. The trail is rocky, for this is a glacial gorge with plenty of climbing, and hidden roots to stub the toe. We cast from the shore or from little "bugs" of paired logs thrown out at the head of the pool; with the trees at our back we have to take care to keep the backcast clear of the evergreens. It is a tingling business, the more so when a fish has followed your fly and may do so again in an unpredictable second. You hear and feel your heart beat, and the tension makes you a little queasy in the pit of your stomach. When he comes and your rod bows to the sudden strike of his power, you are possessed by two instincts, the killer and the lover. And when he leaps clear in his first swift run and you see his shining strength, the blue water, and the band of dark trees, you know that this is what you have been anticipating, this is why you have come.

After luncheon we nap and for an hour and a half the strings of tension are untied. And then it is as if we awakened to a second day. Again, I hear the "Peabody,

Peabody" call of the whitethroat. Again I lie still, reflecting, anticipating, saying to myself "Counting this evening, we have six and a half days of this left. Boy!" Then I tighten the belt and go out.

Emerson had felt all this and he wrote about it in his essay on Nature:

> The tempered light of the woods is like a perpetual morning, and is stimulating and heroic. The anciently-reported spells of these places creep on us. The stems of pines, hemlocks, and oaks almost gleam like iron on the excited eye. The incommunicable trees begin to persuade us to live with them and quit our life of solemn trifles. . . . How easily we might walk onward into the opening landscape, absorbed by new pictures and by thoughts fast succeeding each other, until by degrees the recollection of home was crowded out of the mind, all memory obliterated by the tyranny of the present, and we were led in triumph by nature.

It is our dearest wish to keep the Northwest Miramichi as unspoiled as it is today. Thus far the only commerce to affect it has been that of the lumberman and the set-nets, and the hunter. The break-up of the ice and the spring drive of the logs make noticeable changes in the river bed, deepening some pools, filling in others. The forest feeds the stream, and when blight devastates the spruce here the river becomes vulnerable to the fast run-offs. The Northwest, like so many other Canadian rivers, lays bare the mineral deposits: this year new claims have been staked and prospectors have paddled past us with their samples. Does this portend new roads, new settlements, more changes?

The North Woods

Our camp is one hundred miles from the mouth of the river, and the salmon who leap our falls on their way upstream are making for the redds, their spawning grounds at the headwater. The redds should be out of bounds for all anglers, and those who poach should be penalized, but this is just one of many needed precautions: the trawlers in Miramichi Bay must be restricted or there will be an ever-dwindling run of bright fish; the deep channel — salmon like all big fish avoid the shallows — or at least a portion of it, must be kept free of set-nets. On some stretches as little as 30 per cent of the entire river width is unnetted, except on Sunday when the nets are up. The balance of nature *must be maintained,* and this is better understood in Canada than anywhere with us, though how to enforce it leads to heated argument at Ottawa. By the balance I mean this: that of the fish returning each year to their native river, say approximately four thousand as an average run, an uninjured majority must be preserved to reach the spawning grounds, deposit their eggs, and eventually return to sea. It is the truest of paradoxes that the devoted angler grows to be more concerned with preservation than with the kill. There are many things to think about when you try to protect the river, and there are too few citizens like Dr. J. A. M. Bell of Fredericton, who never ceases thinking about how to do so. Great surgeon that he is, Alec has fought many times to save a life and no less tenaciously to protect the river that he loves. Would there were more like him!

30
Our Secret Neighbors

I have envied but never acquired the habit of the daily diarist. This I regret, for an editor is involved in a network of human relations, and the nature of his calling admits to intimacy as deep and varied as that of the family doctor.

But I do keep a record of expeditions to the woods and streams. Some of the entries, as of my surf-casting for striped bass (one hundred hours of fishing for each striper beached is a fair estimate), are monotonously brief. Others, of our ten days' fishing for salmon on the Northwest Miramichi, are chronicles (complete except for the last day) retaining something of the anticipation, the family banter, the setbacks and the excitement — records my mind will reach back for in the coldness of winter. With these each year I keep a list of Wildlife Seen with the naked eye and without the aid of field glasses.

The list is usually headed by the white-throated sparrow, the herald of the Canadian woods, whose call is the first you hear as you follow the guide up the tote road to camp. Then, when I am in luck, there will be at least one reference to an eagle. This year I saw a superb golden eagle — saw him first (through glasses) perched like a sentinel on the gaunt dead tree above his nest on a high shoulder in the Dartmouth Grants; saw him closer, winging no more than twenty-five yards overhead, as we pulled our canoe in off the Dead Diamond at dusk. Always there is the spruce partridge, the fool hen, shooing her chicks off the path like a distracted housewife, or eying you in supposed concealment as she sits in full view on her spruce stump.

Her brisker cousin the ruffed grouse is a lady of quality. One morning last July, I arrived at Basin Pool only to discover that I had left my dry flies in camp. My wife and the guide had gone on to the top of the Falls, so leaning my rod against a spruce crotch I hurried back down the trail to retrieve those flies, and was armed only with my light rainproof jacket, which I had in my hand. I was traveling quietly, and it was not until I was right beside the spring hole that I was heard and seen by the family of baby partridges who set up an anguish of piping. Up the trail like an arrow came the hen. There wasn't time for any broken-wing decoy, and in fury she drove at my legs. I retreated, and using my windbreaker as a cape in the best Belmonte style, I diverted her to one side. Back she came in another rush, and again the cape turned her aside. Meanwhile I was talking to her in what I intended to be a cajoling tone of voice. Seeing that his wife was still alive, the cock now appeared, and he was something to look at with his scarlet eye and his black and white ruff. They joined forces, and although I had never heard of an angler being pecked to death, it seemed as if this might turn out to be the first time.

Our Secret Neighbors

"Don't be silly," I kept saying, as I warded them off with the windbreaker, "I am not going to hurt you. Get along into the woods."

The chicks had already scurried uphill, and at last the parents followed. But the mother still wasn't sure. She paused for a moment on a dead log as if to launch herself on one last assault. "Go on, old lady," I said, "you're a good girl."

The kingfisher denouncing our invasion of his water; the night hawk swooping for insects over the Home Pool after sunset; the trees from which the bear has torn the bark in his search for grubs; the moose prints in the beaver marsh; the snowshoe hare with lugubrious feet; the little brown bear in George's trap, and Alma, George's daughter, crying, "Kill him quickly, Daddy! Kill him quickly!"; the doe that comes down across the river for her evening salad; the raven devouring a grilse which had been stranded in a shallow pool — these are incidents common enough in any forest which one from the suburbs travels far to see. The pity of it is that one has to travel farther and farther to find such secret places. The jeep, the plane, and the ever-extending roads are penning the wildlife into smaller and smaller pockets.

After the spell of New Brunswick we return to our country cottage, only twenty-seven miles from the center of Boston, with a new sense of companionship. I counted myself lucky to be on hand when a hawk which sometimes scours our woods was set upon by a pack of irate small birds; the bully shed feathers in his hurried retreat and I have one of them in my fishing hat. Our summer cottage in its three acres of woods adjoins a sprawling, undeveloped, largely uncut estate of some two thousand acres, with ponds and unvisited rocky lairs, and so we enjoy the benefit of a preserve.

In the pine woods on the ridge above us is where Raccy and his family lived. Two summers ago in the early morning hours we heard through our sleep the clanging-to of the iron cover of our underground garbage container, and in the daylight was the clear evidence that someone was helping himself. A smart dog, we thought, though could he really press down on the pedal that raises the lid? The visitor, growing bolder, kept coming earlier, until one night my wife stationed herself behind the door with a flashlight. When the lid clanged she darted out on the back porch and aimed the beam at the bin. Nothing was there. She covered every shadow within the small enclosure — the place was deserted; and as she raised the light, there on the top of the fence four feet away sat a big raccoon, smiling, his tail gently weaving.

That first summer Raccy came as the light faded on the long June evenings. There is a small window at the midpoint of our cellar stairs, and sitting there in the fading light we could watch him get his hands under the lid and then brace with his hindquarters as he forced his head and shoulders in; he'd take his time choosing his delicacies, tossing them out, and then in a whisk he'd be gone and the lid would clang.

We felt that things could be put on a friendlier basis if we knew what he relished. We could tell from the litter the morning after what it was he disdained: tea bags, eggshells, orange rinds, stale cake were obvious discards. What he favored were bits of fish, bacon rind, meat, fat of any kind, French bread, and best of all, the shells and stomachs of lobster. We found this by tracing him to the little pool in the rock garden; here he evidently dunked his trophies before he ate them and then departed, leaving the fragments on the edge.

We thought to bring him closer by leaving a coffee-can half-full of bacon fat at the top of the kitchen steps. That he enjoyed it, we knew next day, from the tiny, greasy fingerprints on the wood. But the coffee-can had disappeared, not in the pool, not anywhere — and it was two weeks before we spotted it at the base of a big, blasted pine on the ridge — a quarter of a mile distant — and so knew that we were at Raccy's door.

In July he brought his wife along and we who were watching saw the blur of the second furry body as she dropped from the fence. He showed her how to force up the iron lid and growled her away from his first handfuls. But when she came to try, she lacked his strength, lost control and down came the cover pinching her paws. She let out a little, whirring protest and waved her hands in the air like a boy who has hit his thumb with a hammer.

Now, growing familiar, he came at dusk; and once, being detected, he scooted for cover behind the fence — all but the bushy tail, which continued in full view. In his haste he had dropped the fat he had been carrying. "Raccy, don't be foolish," said my wife gently; "come back and get it." At which point he emerged in full view, came up the steps, retrieved his dainty with a bland look on his painted mask, and then streaked off for the rock garden.

It got so when we heard the lid clang we'd grin at each other and say "Our friends." Then one evening in early August we heard enough commotion to bring us to the back porch. Raccy was not in the enclosure, but we could hear him muttering in the gloaming. And something certainly was in the container. Ted stepped on the pedal, the lid flew up; and there, head and tiny paws appearing, was the boldest of the cubs. He climbed out and, tail waving, went up to Ted, stood up on his hind legs and reached his tiny paws placatingly towards Ted's knee as if to say "O.K.? O.K.?" Then he moved to my wife, and made the same friendly gesture. Overhead the whickering had increased and, looking up, we saw the black and white heads of three other cubs peering down at us from the pine branches. Meantime Junior had joined the Old Man. This was the first time, as you might say, the two families met.

We have other neighbors not so regular in their visits. I enjoy the gray squirrel scampering over our bedroom roof; the bright-eyed chipmunk who flickers in and out of his hole in the stone foundation only a step away from the screen door; even the rabbits who eat the heads of our zinnias — never my idea of a luscious flower; most of all the deer, so unexpected in this settled countryside, who up to this spring have left their imprint in the soft mud of our courtyard.

But the neighborhood is changing fast: a new two-lane highway has bulldozed its way through the finest woods in Essex County and now passes within half a mile of our ridge. Already the pastel-tinted string towns are springing up, and soon we shall have more dogs and cats, more children — a total of more neighbors, but far fewer of the secret sort.

V
Home

31
Mickey

OVERHEAD the oak leaves stir against the cloudless blue, and the shadow in which I am reading ripples like running water. At my feet on the borderline between the sunny and the cool grass lies Mickey dozing, gray muzzle pointed toward the driveway up which the family will return from their expedition. Periodically he rouses himself, shakes the catkins from his black curls, and moves closer to the sun. His movement renews the scolding of the mother robin in the bittersweet and interrupts my intake of print. I watch him, and through the forming impressions of the book in my lap, memory thrusts its feeling.

This is probably our last summer together. Mickey is sixteen and that is a great age for a cocker spaniel given to eating any old thing; indeed a great age for any dog. Implicit in every friendship is the trust that it will never break. Mick has no reason to doubt us, but we who note his fading hearing and his inability to spot us at any distance on the beach live with the warning to make these months good.

I remember William Morton Wheeler's remarking on the silent communication between dogs, and how, when he had taken one of his for a walk through the Arboretum, the others would gather about the traveler instantly on his return and by scent and emanation have all the news in a matter of seconds. On the Common with other dogs Mick is eager, quivering, and gregarious when I am along, and hair-on-end belligerent when accompanying his mistress. In canine years he is now well past the century mark, so it is small wonder that dogs in their prime have only a passing curiosity in what he has to say. They pause, there is the usual tail-wagging introduction. Then, while he is still standing on his dignity, they suddenly lope off. Mick will start after and then resign himself to his own grass, which he scratches up with a "What the hell." For ladies he has, I gather, the charm of an aging colonel. There is a honey-colored spaniel who, after the nosing, will describe mad circles about him as he stands immovable on the moonlit Common. But if she pushes him too roughly he loses his balance and shows his lip, and so they part.

At home his expressions are stressed for our benefit. His humor, as when with jaws open and tongue half a yard out he stands there grinning; his sneeze of expectation; his mutter — a kind of controlled yip — of annoyance; his jumping recognition of those most important words in a city dog's vocabulary, "Going out" and "Down country" (is it the special note that colors our voices as we say them?); his sharp demanding bark when his water dish is empty or when brownies, his passion, are cooking — these are a language no one could miss. So too his boredom when, after a decent interval in our friend's house, he fetches his leash and stands obdurate with it in his jaws.

And in his play, he loves to tease. Mickey came to us

[200]

Mickey

when he was three weeks old and in the pecking order he established himself as a contemporary of my daughter Sara and as a senior in every respect to young Ted. In his youth we spent the winters in an apartment on the Fenway, and here Mickey devised a series of games for his own and our amusement. There was one he liked to play with a Malaga grape. A grape would be given him and he would go through the motions of chewing it. Then he would lie down facing us, his head cocked on one side. With a sudden twist he would fling the grape, perfectly intact, over his shoulder and pounce upon it as it rolled along the rug or under the table. Again the mock seriousness of swallowing it, the fixed stare in our direction, and again, the quick projection. The wonder was that he could keep this up for such a long time without puncturing the thin-skinned grape.

He loved to tease Sara about her dollhouse. The open rooms were just right for his inspection, and the inmates — known as Mr. and Mrs. Brewster — were much to his taste. He would stand gazing into the living room until he was sure Sara was watching him; then with a quick dart he would seize one of the little dolls and be off, up the hall, through the kitchen, through the dining room, across the living room, and into the hall again. It was a lovely circle, and Sara could seldom catch him without the help of May, the cook. Sara's revenge was unpremeditated. One evening she set Mr. and Mrs. Brewster at the dinner table and served each of them a chocolate-covered Ex-lax for their supper, and after she had gone to sleep Mickey ate both. On rising the next morning, I found

[201]

that he used the bathroom in a hurry, and Sara, all unknowing, supplied the perfect caption at breakfast: "Now, Mother, I told you the dolls were alive. They ate their candy."

I remember those times when he seemed to speak my language, once for instance when in his puppyhood he was sick from a distemper injection. He began vomiting at midnight and at four I got the car and drove him to the vet's. He was so weak that he leaned limply against the corner of seat and door, but in answer to my hand his eyes said, "I'm sorry to be such a mess. But I *am* sick." And again, years later, when he had to apologize for his hunting. It was summer and our little cottage adjoined the orchard and vegetable garden of our big neighbor. At sundown rabbits would make free with the tender lettuce and carrots, and their scent — when Mickey got it — drove him wild. One evening from our screened porch I spotted a cottontail in the green. Mick was asleep, but quietly opening the door I pointed him at the quarry and he got the idea. Rabbit and spaniel disappeared over the horizon with yips marking every second bound. Two hours went by, and then in darkness there was Mick scratching at the screen. "No luck," he said, and in his mouth was the half-eaten carrot the rabbit had dropped in his haste. "No luck."

Mickey is by his nature a hunter and a retriever. But now, with his teeth gone, his retrieving is limited to fishermen's corks as they curve ahead of him on the beach, and to apples in the orchard. He fancied himself a hunter, and for years he nourished a grudge against squirrels. I used to tease him about this. Walking close to one of our oaks, I would peer up into the leaves and touch the bark significantly; whereupon Mick would leave the ground jumping and scrabbling as high as my arm.

The squirrels, for their part, enjoyed the feud: they knew he could never catch them. I remember one summer day when Mickey was lying on the open porch soaking up the sun which radiated from the warm boards. Close to the house stood an old apple tree, one of whose branches reached over the porch. Along this bridge, as Mickey slept, stole one of his bushy-tailed enemies. With mathematical precision the squirrel nipped clean a hard green apple, which hit the porch with a thump an inch from Mickey's nose. It was as nice a piece of natural comedy as I have ever witnessed; and the aftermath was noisy.

That dogs remember, we know from their habits and from their twitching dreams when they are so palpably reliving some activity. But how far back does their memory reach, and do those little half-uttered cries indicate that, like man, they are long haunted by old fears? If so, then Mick may still feel the most painful terror of domesticated animals — the fear of desertion. The autumn of his second year, my wife and I had to answer a sudden call to New York. We closed the cottage, packed up the daughter, and to save time left the pup with the maid. She took him to her home in Watertown, and from it he naturally escaped in search of us. That was on Friday afternoon. They saw him for an instant at the garbage pail Saturday morning, and then he was gone for good.

By our return on Monday there wasn't a clue. We drove the unfamiliar streets and we put our appeal in the newspapers and on the air. In twenty-four hours we had heard from seventeen spaniel owners, fifteen of whom had lost their own dogs. But one of them gave us a tip. In their search they had seen a small black dog in the vast reaches of the Watertown Arsenal. So, with the Governor's permission, we drove through the gates — this was long before the war — to explore the cement strips which led between the huge closed buildings. A sergeant's son gave us hope. "Sure," he said, "a little black dog. He's here all right, only you can't get close to him." "Don't scare him," I said. "Find him if you can." Whistling and calling, we went to point after point, and once on the knoll above a huge oil tank I thought I heard the short familiar bark, but nothing moved. Three hours later we came back to the same spot, and there was the boy lying full-length on the cement wall aiming an imaginary gun. "The buffalo is down here," he called. Ten yards farther, and I saw Mick's nest and his unmistakable head. "Mickey," I shouted. Then up the slope he came on the dead run, his ears brown pancakes of burr.

Is it the fear of our leaving him that so troubles him when he can now no longer hear us as we move about the house? The sight of an open suitcase makes him more doleful than does a thunderstorm. When we pack for the country there is no way to tell him that he will surely come too. In his heart of hearts Mick knows that he is de-

pendent upon four people, and no comfort of maid or sit-
ter can distract his vigil when we are gone for the evening. Our woods are his woods. The squirrels who used to
scold him he no longer hears. He begins not to hear us.
But we shall hear him long after he is gone.

32
Blizzard in Boston

THE windows of my *Atlantic* office look over the most vivacious acres of cultivated oystershell in New England — I mean the Boston Public Garden — so that, as I read or dictate, my gaze is occasionally arrested by the antics of the Back Bay canines (many of them made known to me by Mickey), or of the children, in their bright worsteds, skating and tumbling on the frozen pond. Today as I worked, my senses kept reporting the blizzard's progress: in the mind's ear I noted the soft announcement of the first theme as the tiny particles, widely spaced, drifted down from the leaden sky; then the snowfall was joined by the sea winds sweeping in from the harbor; the tempo rose, pedestrians tucked in their chins and braced themselves against the slanting white arrows. For a capricious interval the wind fell and the flakes were heavy, fantastic goblets.

Then we passed into the blue dusk, and as we goose-stepped our first footprints into the white paths, homeward bound, we could see the aureole of the arc lights the whirling haze which needled our faces and deepened the drifts.

There are distinct movements and melodies in this tone

poem of Snow in Town. The jingle of bells one no longer hears, nor the whine of iron-rimmed wagon wheels on dry-packed roads — the milk wagon at dawn. But against the hush of the white blanket other sounds stand out: the scrape of snow shovels against the uneven bricks; the click, rhythm, and bite of the tire chains; the rumble and thud of snow falling from the gabled roofs; horns hooting as harassed motorists line up for home, the shrill of the traffic whistle and, at intervals, the crash of fender and bumper as cars collide.

Snow provides its local comedy and strife. Snow fights have been waged on Boston Common ever since the eighteenth century: the redcoats — the "lobster backs" — must have been a tempting target during the occupation, and after their departure the warfare went on between the North-Enders and the West-Enders. In the *Education* Henry Adams gives us his unforgettable account of a fight in which he took part almost a century ago:

Whenever, on a half-holiday, the weather was soft enough to soften the snow, the Common was apt to be the scene of a fight, which began in daylight with the Latin School in force, rushing their opponents down to Tremont Street, and which generally ended at dark by the Latin School dwindling in numbers and disappearing. As the Latin School grew weak, the roughs and young blackguards grew strong. As long as snowballs were the only weapon, no one was much hurt, but a stone may be put in a snowball, and in the dark a stick or a slingshot in the hands of a boy is as effective as a knife. One afternoon the fight had been long and exhausting. The boy Henry, following, as his habit was, his bigger brother

Charles, had taken part in the battle, and had felt his courage much depressed by seeing one of his trustiest leaders, Henry Higginson — "Bully Hig," his school name — struck by a stone over the eye, and led off the field bleeding in rather a ghastly manner. As night came on, the Latin School was steadily forced back to the Beacon Street Mall where they could retreat no further without disbanding, and by that time only a small band was left, headed by two heroes, Savage and Marvin. A dark mass of figures could be seen below, making ready for the last rush, and rumor said that a swarm of blackguards from the slums, led by a grisly terror called Conky Daniels, with a club and a hideous reputation, was going to put an end to the Beacon Street cowards forever. Henry wanted to run away with the others, but his brother was too big to run away, so they stood still and waited immolation. The dark mass set up a shout, and rushed forward. The Beacon Street boys turned and fled up the steps, except Savage and Marvin and the few champions who would not run. The terrible Conky Daniels swaggered up, stopped a moment with his body-guard to swear a few oaths at Marvin, and then swept on and chased the flyers, leaving the few boys untouched who stood their ground. The obvious moral taught that blackguards were not so black as they were painted. . . .

Fortunately for the pedestrian the snowballing is no longer as regimented as this, now that the town has grown larger, but the sniping goes on, behind trees and up the slopes of Monument Hill.

Our corner at Arlington and Marlborough is one of the slipperiest in all Boston when there is ice under the snow. From my window one winter's noon, I remember watching a man in a big fur coat as he stepped off the curb head down against the snow. I saw the taxi before he did, and the taxi driver saw him. In his panic Mr. Fur Coat lost his balance and fell flat. The driver slammed on his brakes and went into one of those unbelievable skids. Taxi and bumper came slithering toward the recumbent figure. "Throw up your legs," shouted the driver. The man threw up his legs, caught his heels on the bumper, and was pushed like a snowplow into the middle of Arlington Street. There the car stopped. The driver helped up Fur Coat, brushed him off, and didn't even charge him a quarter for the ride.

Snow has a way of catching you unaware. After a February blizzard, to step out of doors into the dazzling glare of the cold morning light, to feel the intense contrast of the sunshine and shadow, to draw the tonic of the winter air into nostril and throat, is to get the full charge of New England. As I was starting off dazed and tingling one morning I paused, swept off my hat, and made a sweeping bow to my wife and daughter, framed in the dining-room window. At that moment, while I was in my courtly posture, head bent and hat in hand, the roof let go its overnight accumulation of frosted snow, and for a moment I was lost in a white cloud. When the avalanche was over I went back into the house, rough-toweled my head, and put on a fresh shirt, trying not to listen to the whoops of glee belowstairs.

Blizzards that last through the night will occasionally paralyze the city. We wake to see the snowfall driven in slanting surges by the north wind, a few humped cars drifted in by the curb, and nothing moving. The children have already been listening to the radio and the refrain, repeated over and over, "No school, all schools, all day! No school, all schools, all day!" has given them the liberation they were hoping for. I know that the elderly members of our staff will not try to reach the office, and my thoughts go back to the early 20's when dear old Miss Emery, our white-haired proofreader, used to face the snowy, slippery mornings, her feet strapped to what looked to me like small iron-shod hoofs: "ground-grippers" they were called. Now, there seems to be no sign of let-up and there is something comforting in the thought that we are being shut in by the white blanket and there is nothing we can do about it.

It is very rare to have the town completely snowbound; indeed I have only known it to happen twice in thirty years. Snowdrifts twelve feet deep and paths across the Common between banks shoulder-high are an old wives' tale in Boston. But I remember the next thing to it in 1939. The schools were closed, the subway and busses were stopped, commuters were warned to stay at home, even the mechanical snowplows could not get their teeth in at first. The storm which had been pelting us for more than twenty-four hours began to let up at eleven in the morning and the sun broke through. On Beacon Hill we neighbors stepped out into a silent, blinding-white city. There was no business and no traffic. We chatted as we dug ourselves out and the snowbanks were higher than our kids. Mickey, who loved to charge into snow nose-down, had to heave himself into leaps like a black rabbit when we took him into the unchanneled Public Garden.

Blizzard in Boston

A policeman stationed himself at the corner of Mount Vernon and Charles Streets — Charles had not yet been cleared for cars — and this was the first and only time I have seen Flexible Flyers and skiers taking the long coast down the fine slope of Mount Vernon Street. Oh, it was a happy interval, and even as it happened we had the feeling it was one of those things that never occurred except in "the good old days."

33
Beacon Hill

BEACON HILL is a village within a city; it is the highest of the hills on which Boston was originally built, and it takes its name from the flaming beacon which was set alight in the early times to guide skippers into the dark harbor. On the slopes of the Hill stand those rose-brick houses built some before some after the Revolution which give this high point of Boston its indestructible beauty.

Mt. Vernon Street, where stand the oldest homes, showing the genius of Bulfinch and the Adam brothers; Chestnut Street, whose graceful fanlights and famous doorways were admired before the War of 1812; West Cedar Street with its grillework and iron balconies; Revere Street with its tiny hidden courts like Sentry Hill Place; Louisburg Square, which is thought by some to be more English than England itself and where the carolers sing on Christmas Eve — these are the veins of the Hill and Charles Street is its main artery.

Charles Street, which lies at the foot of Beacon Hill, is that unique blend of the past and the present which you rarely find in America. The shops on either side were once substantial residences — you can see that from the archi-

[212]

tecture of the upper stories; here lived state governors, famous historians, and charming hostesses like Mrs. James T. Fields, with whom Dickens and Thackeray, Bret Harte and Mark Twain used to visit.

Sometimes an old mansion gives way to a newcomer like the most popular restaurant on the Hill, owned by our Bostonian from Greece, Mr. Stavros. Here, in these servantless days, old Boston forgathers for lunch before the Symphony — the Boston Symphony, of course; here, on the off-beat hours, the taxi drivers eat; and here drama students, secretaries, and nurses from the Massachusetts General Hospital argue about the Red Sox or modern art, as dark-eyed Sam Demas serves up lamb hearts, chops or the delectable custard rice pudding.

Take time to poke around on Charles Street. Talk to Mrs. Fishelson, who with her husband operates the loveliest flower shop east of San Francisco. Mrs. Fishelson is from Paris; the flowers respond to her Gallic temperament, and their color lights up our whole street. She is spunky as a terrier, but when France fell she was disconsolate, and took to her bed and was eventually taken to the hospital. On the third day, so she told me, the doctor said to her, "So you won't get up? But it isn't going to change anything in France if you stay in bed all your life. It's up to you." Up she got and in three months was beginning to plan for the shipments of food and drugs which she sent over to those in the Resistance.

Mrs. Fishelson has dancing black eyes and the best Gallic wit on the Street. Her flowers obey her. They are spick-and-span, heads up, and in full blaze. The doors of her shop are always open, the pots and flowering shrubs reaching toward the air, toward your eyes, toward your pocketbook. She was walking briskly along Charles Street one day with a friend of mine when she encountered Lady Bountiful. "Oh, Mrs. Fishelson," said the Lady, "that arrangement you made for me was so lovely — you know, it won Second Prize at the Show." Mrs. Fishelson thanked her and turned into her shop, my friend with her. "Did you also arrange the First Prize?" asked my friend. "Yes, of course," said Mrs. Fishelson.

Diagonally opposite the Fishelsons' is the fruit shop and delicatessen which for a long time was presided over by Mrs. DeLuca. She and her dark-eyed Joe came to Charles Street years ago and with the taste and energy of Italy they began to build up a fruit shop — fresh fruit from California, Florida, and Georgia, good groceries and good cheese for the Bohemians on the back side of the Hill, snacks at almost any time of the day and night sold cheerfully in a shop where in zero weather you could see your breath. Rumor had it that there was no furnace, nor would the owner install one, but Mrs. DeLuca, with her black shawl over her shoulders, was always there generating warmth and ready for any emergency. During the war one of our *grandes dames* came clumping in with her stick to order barley flour and dried peas. "No barley flour and no dried peas," said Mrs. DeLuca. "What," said the *grande dame,* "no barley flour and dried peas? What *is* the world coming to?"

When the DeLuca cat (for whom Mickey has a blustering respect) had kittens, my wife naturally asked how many there were. "Why, she's a society woman," said Mrs. DeLuca, "she never has more than one at a time."

The DeLucas slaved and saved for twenty-seven years to buy their part of the block; and we were proud of them when the sale went through for $80,000.

Next door to them is our corner druggist, Clough and Shackley, whose prescription book goes back to 1848; chat with Mr. McLellan, the druggist-historian-owner; ask him to show you the cow lane which still gives every Beacon Hiller the right-of-way to lead a cow *through* Beacon Street to the Common.

Charles Street has more curiosity shops per square foot than any other thoroughfare in North America. The stock of these antique shops, if Texas decided to buy them out all at once, would run into the millions — brass andirons, leather firebuckets, grandfather clocks, weathervanes, old brass in a hundred patterns, Sandwich glass, Duncan Phyfe, and tea sets in copper luster.

Take Mr. Finnerty — or let him take you in a friendly deal. Not long ago Mr. Finnerty and his rival, Mrs. Grossman, were viewing the ruins of a magnificent highboy which had come down from Portsmouth. The barbarian who had previously owned it had sawed off its four legs, so there sat the beautiful highboy squat on the floor of the shop. And there stood the two dealers venting their indignation. "Well," said Mr. Finnerty, "I hope the blankety-blank saw slipped and took off *his* legs, too!" Mr. Finnerty, like all fine craftsmen, is a perfectionist. "I don't mind an honest reproduction," he once told my wife, "but, Lord, how I hate a fake."

Home

Along Charles Street walk the ghosts of those who once owned or used these things — Governor Andrew, Francis Parkman, Longfellow, Emerson and Lowell, Mr. and Mrs. Fields, Oliver Wendell Holmes — a host of distinguished names of American history.

But this is not a museum. Streets like Charles Street of Beacon Hill are the arteries of American life. They are the living proof of our heritage and of our democracy.

34
The War against Paper

IN this world of ours where things are in the saddle and ride mankind, so many of us are slaves. There are women who are enslaved to money or clothes or society, and men who are enslaved to their business, to their law practice or doctoring, to their passion for ticker tapes and bonds and shares. I too am a slave to paper, but of a different kind. This has developed some peculiar habits in the Weeks family.

As an undergraduate editor thirty-five years ago, I first found myself possessed by a love of the printed word, and an ever-increasing respect for manuscripts. I religiously kept all my own young themes — I have them still — and this habit of acquisition has grown on me with the years. A neat man but never quite so orderly as I intend to be, I collect papers of all sorts. I collect letters from our authors and find it hard to destroy the more affectionate ones from my family. I collect old golf scores and Christmas cards; I must have thirty pounds of lectures written in longhand, committed to memory but not destroyed; I cut out editorials and news articles which have hit me as farsighted; I bring home Commencement programs and menus of banquets I have enjoyed, and the programs of

"First Nights"; and clippings about a certain editor and his magazine — clippings which have long since overflowed the wooden file given me by a harassed housewife one Christmas.

As I have said, I am a neat man. But the problem of where to put all this paper is something which overwhelms my sense of order. Each night before going to bed I collect the papers from my pockets and place them on the mantel in my bedroom. Some of these return to the office with me the following morning. Most do not. Gradually the pyramid grows, and when it threatens to spill on the floor, I put a book on top of it.

This is a danger signal which my mentor is quick to recognize. "Mrs. Gordon," she says, "is dusting the room today, and I won't have those damn papers on the mantel for another minute." Habit has made me resigned to this, but as I thumb through the pyramid, being careful not to let it slither on the floor, which would give the mentor a laugh, I say to myself, "Never have I had a desk big enough for what I need! Never have I had the place for papers a literary man needs!" I stuff the papers away in one of the drawers in my closet — the one which still has some room in it.

The trouble is paper breeds so rapidly. With the help of John Dewey and Charles A. Beard, I compiled a list of the Most Influential Books published over the last century. The list was taken up by the press. There were editorials and syndicated articles, clippings from the four corners. They still come in from the clipping bureau, and where to keep them!

The War Against Paper

Another trouble is that my mentor keeps raiding my piles. She long ago began to run her life by lists, and my envelopes give her just the memorandum space she needs. So she will snake one of the envelopes out of my pile and on the back of it will write these cabalistic symbols: —

Mrs. Clark telephone
Doorbell no ring
Mrs. Brown & Mr. Weiner
  Box of clothes
  Sheets and parachute
Dentist
Pierce canapés Gin
Linoleum plastic fur coat
Permanent

The list is supposed to do its duty propped up against the mirror of her dressing table, and if, as sometimes happens, I reclaim the envelope for my own and walk it back to the office, there are mutual recriminations.

Every now and then there is an outburst in our war against paper. The virus of house cleaning suddenly enters the mind, and the time for action is Now. The mentor upbraids me for the manuscripts I have left in my little library, for the mass of clippings and correspondence not put away. I retaliate by jerking open her desk drawer and pointing to the unanswered invitations, the unopened appeals — and the bills.

For a change I led the assault, on a rainy Saturday not long ago. "Here we are," I said, "supposed to be responsible people, and look at that drawer — invitations not answered, donations not sent, bills not paid. Have you finished the Christmas letters? And how about the Hemplewhite wedding?" I continued, opening the fat expensive envelope. "Do you know which one of their daughters this is? If we're going, for the Lord's sake let's write the acceptance and send a little present. Ash trays." At this point with silent fury my mentor took over.

That was on Saturday. Wednesday evening came a telephone call. Mrs. Hemplewhite. "Ted," she said, "could it be that you and Fritzy were planning to come to Dorothy's wedding?" "Yes," I replied, and my voice was eager, for here I knew we had done our duty. "We are looking forward to it with pleasure." "But Ted," she said, "the wedding was two years ago. Dorothy will love the ash trays. But I thought you knew that she just had her second baby."

It is hard to blush over the telephone, but I did. Then I came back to the mentor. "How did you dream it out? Whatever made you keep that envelope for two years?" "Well," she said primly, "I thought it was the best-looking wedding invitation we had ever received. I was keeping it as a model when time came for Sara's wedding."

35
Hurricane

WE have a fair stand of oaks that covers the path leading up to the top of our ridge, but just before the crest and extending for a mile along the plateau on top is a pine woods. The oldest pine which I have measured with the Thoreau embrace (with both arms outstretched it takes two and a half hugs) I reckon to be more than a century old; and because of a hornlike broken limb low down, it is known as the Rhino Pine. The juniors are well spaced, with the brown carpet beneath them making for easy rambles. Not a few of the oldest are at least a hundred, and except for an occasional windfall and one lightning-struck veteran, they are a well-preserved grove. Are — or rather, were.

For five months of the year my Kerry Blue, Desmond, and I frequent the pines at least once a day. The length of the expedition varies with the time and light, for I am a commuter and many a day we do not enter the sanctuary until the golden or bronze dusk. But whatever the hour, there are certain way stations where we pause for reflection. These include the open knoll where Desmond sometimes doses himself with dyspepsia grass; the half-overturned rusty stump which the raccoons keep pushing into for grubs; the hollow tree which we identify as Raccy's apartment house; the pine which was exploded by lightning, where I casually collect the white heartwood scattered in a radius of sixty yards; the swamp, with its dimpling insects and water hyacinths, lying below the old stone wall; and the hawk's nest. I have long known that there was a hawk in residence, but I did not discover the nest until Desmond discovered the squirrel corpse beneath it. These are our habitual observation points, and there may be other pauses when we see deer prints, hear the owl or kingfisher, or when Desmond is examining scents far beyond my detection, or suddenly tearing off in one of those great circles which are his way of expressing exuberance.

It was refreshing and lovely and it seemed permanent. Of all growing things, a tree is the most nearly immortal. The great ones like the Rhino Pine, so scarred and weather-beaten, yet green of top, are the epitome of ruggedness. Seeing them unchanged year after year gives us the illusion that we ourselves change little. To walk in this pine woods was to find tranquillity, though for reasons I never stopped to realize until it was too late. These evenly spaced boles with their canopy meeting overhead stood for order and calm; the path we had worn in the pine needles opened up continual vistas through which the soft shafts of sunlight illuminated a small, calm universe. All of us who walk for thought have our secret places which invite the mind. This was mine.

Everything about a hurricane is deadly to trees rooted on a northern moraine: the hours of torrential rain which weakens their foothold, and then the wind, gusty at first, but turning in on itself, as the eye of the storm approaches, so that the heavily leaved trees are wrenched and twisted in their self-defense. In 1938 the cruelest blows came late in the afternoon and lasted into the dark, but in Carol and in Edna — what effeminate names for such havoc! — the damage was done in daylight. An oak fighting for its life and without enough soil to hold it would lose its top or a great limb would crack, would dangle and then be stripped off. When the screaming velocity rose above 80 m.p.h. and our nerves told us we were close to the eye, we could see and hear the pines going down. Death came in two ways: the older trees, already somewhat rotted at the core, as the autopsy revealed, were snapped off anywhere from four to twenty feet from the ground; those still sound pulled out the great mushroom of the roots and went down like ninepins, carrying smaller trees under them as they fell. So they lie today, in windrows and crisscrossed, body on top of body, as though pushed down by a giant thumb.

For two days there were no birds to be seen: they had found refuge in thickets and were not yet venturing forth; when at last they emerged, the hawks — not one but three — were gliding more boldly than I have ever seen before, and the small birds did not gang up against them. Wasps and bees were everywhere; their nests destroyed, they were angrily invading kitchens, cars, golf courses, as nervous as the rest of us; but the angriest rasp in the air was that of the power saw which echoed from hill to hill as the fallen trees were cut up. This is a loss which cannot be remedied in our lifetime, for the places can never look as they were. The shade trees which were the glory of the North Shore, down; the old elms in the Common and Public Garden, down; the conifers which once made a green wall along Common Lane, down; the elms on Coolidge Point, down; the forest plantings which Olmsted laid out on Moraine Farm back in the eighties, down; the oaks in the Arnold Arboretum, down. Whether it was the show place, the village green, the quiet wood, or the suburban maple which screened your porch from the neighbor's — these are what we have lost and will long remember.

36
The Open Heart

As we settle back into our private lives, the guard goes up. Reticence has returned. I see it as I travel. I miss the camaraderie, the sharing, the boy picked up as he thumbed his way back from leave, the friendliness which so often led to unburdening. I miss the candor and the heart with which Americans turned to each other while the pressure was on.

This feeling of unanimity grew on us by degrees. I felt it on my trip across the continent in February, 1942, particularly in San Francisco, which was then receiving the first wounded. The war came home to San Francisco early, and in that heavenly room which hangs like a lantern above the Golden Gate, the Top of the Mark, — to the north one could see the submarine net and to the south the first transports making up for Australia, — I watched men and women in uniform, strangers sizing each other up, not critically as in civilian life, but with a sense of belonging. The guards were down.

Who can forget the patience and the humor of the crowds? It was in our railway stations, from the Pennsylvania Terminal to the whistle stops, that you saw character in the open, and the heart on the sleeve. I think of the files of selectees, hatless, leaving one life with no more luggage than a toothbrush — how they would stand there covering up embarrassment with the old horse laugh; and in the shadow and out of touch, the mother with the red eyes, the old man, so inarticulate, and the kid brothers.

I remember one midnight in the Dayton station. Ohio was a bottleneck of shipping at the time and the train was more than two hours late. Information kept repeating, "Twelve thirty-five, yes, twelve thirty-five" — which meant that we'd be sitting up until three fifteen in the morning before we reached Indianapolis. Many of us were waiting — parents who had been seeing their flyers at Wright Field; Army wives with the little kangaroos; salesmen, soldiers, and WAC's. When at last the train did show up, there were extra coaches for our benefit; crowding the aisles and sitting on the arms, we could just fit in.

And then, since sleep was out of the question, a vaudeville show began. The car attendant was a little, very dark Negro with a white smile. He'd edge into the car with something to sell, the salesman nearest the door would nab him, and an auction would begin — pillows, sandwiches, Lily cups of coffee, were auctioned off with some pretty good cracks. As we rattled along there was singing, and when the conductor fought his way in, he really ran the gantlet. The heat, the sprawled, relaxed figures, the lovers, head on shoulder, the merciless light — crude? Sure, crude as Chaucer. But unmistakably American and unanimous.

For the couples those stations must have been unforgettable. South Station, Grand Central, the Union at Washington — who could ever paint, not the uniforms, but the hurry, the tension, and the muteness? You don't speak when you're snatching at time. There aren't words. But the fingers lock and the eyes hold back time in that long utterable look, the look civilians tried not to bump into.

I remember being on a Local which stopped for a century at Salem. Right beneath my window a GI and his wife were looking farewell. They fixed that train, even after the conductor's "All aboard!" had urged him into the seat beside me — it didn't go. The two-year-old was held up to the window and the GI kept looking, and it felt like tearing apart when at last we jerked into motion. When we were safely out of sight his tears came.

I remember an early breakfast in the station at Pittsburgh and a fine-looking woman of about my age who was crying silently as she read a red-and-blue-edged letter. She was not looking at any of us, nor we at her, but the grief was plain and unreticent.

About a year or so later I remember flying north from Alabama. June, the midnight flight, and a moon big as a barn. My seat mate was a sailor home bound from San Diego after fourteen months in the Pacific. "Where you getting off, sailor?" "Charlotte, sir. I live forty miles over the mountain from Charlotte." "Will they be expecting you?" "I sent 'em a wire but I don't reckon they'll get it."

It was 3:00 A.M. when we put our wheels down at Charlotte and he was dead to the world. The stewardess and I shook him. "Sailor, you're home," I said. "No," he mumbled, "wanna get off at Charlotte." Well, we got him to his feet at last — he'd lost his hat — and I followed him down the dimly lit plane to see him ashore. Half drunk with sleep, he tacked across the apron, making for a flight of stairs, and just as he walked into the floodlight a girl in a red dress came down like a diver. "Johnny!" she cried, and the note of her voice I can still hear; then she was in his arms, her feet clean off the ground. I looked up the stairs and there in the shadows were the family, the elders waiting their turn.

We are speaking of the open heart. I don't say this is the way to live — this anguish, this uprooting, this cry of return. I say that while we had to, we lived with the open heart, and with a sympathy for others that makes us a great people. See that we do not close it too soon in our hurry, our reticence or suspicion.

Index

Index

[231]

Index

Index

Index

Index

Index